BUSINESS TRAVEL

CAN BE FUN!

Robert Naggar

Business Travel Can Be Fun - how to Have Fun While you Travel

©2017. Robert Naggar. All Rights Reserved.

No part of this book may be reproduced or transmitted in any form or by any means, electronic or mechanical, including photocopying, recording, or by any information storage and retrieval system without written permission of the publisher.

ISBN: 978-1-936449-94-1 (paperback)

Cover and Interior: Christa E. Kegl

BANYAN·TREE·PRESS
Banyan Tree Press is an imprint of
www.HugoHousePublishers.com
Hugo House Publishers, Ltd.
Denver, Colorado
Austin, Texas
Banyan Tree Press is an imprint of
www.HugoHousePublishers.com

Praise for Business Travel Can Be Fun!

"I've been traveling on business for over forty years and, in the process, have often got upset over all kinds of problems. When I saw this title, I thought Robert Naggar didn't know what business travel was about. This riotus book somewhat changed my outlook. Since reading it, rather than get upset, I try to identify with Naggar's remarkable humor and relaxed style and laugh or smile at most problems. Travel is now, indeed, much more fun!"

Alex Adjemian
Businessman and World
Traveler, Hollywood.

"After reading his book and often laughing out loud in the process, I fully associate with Robert Naggar's "Business travel can be fun". As a world traveler, one cannot avoid problems. I had many and, after looking back on them, I now wish I could have seen them with the same eyes and recount them with the same vivacity and humor as Naggar's prose. An exceptionally funny and enriching book."

Richard Smouha,
Lawyer, investment advisor and
author

"While trawling the Kindle store for something amusing to read on a train journey, I came across Robert Naggar's compilation of humorous short stories about some of his travel experiences during the course of a long business career. I downloaded a sample, but it didn't take long for me to want to buy the book.

"Not just a seasoned traveller, Naggar is also multilingual and knowledgeable about the customs and lifestyles of many of the countries he has visited, which makes the stories informative and interesting as well as funny. I couldn't put the book down until I'd read them all.

"What I enjoyed most was his wicked sense of humour. Some of the absurd experiences he describes are hilarious, all the funnier because they happen to be true. Without being unkind, he doesn't mince his words or give way to political correctness when describing people and situations and I found myself laughing out loud on numerous occasions. His writing is acutely visual which is why the cameos are so situationally comical. If you want a good laugh and an interesting read you will love this book. I did!

Annie Wotton,
MA Applied Linguistics
B Ed Hons Dip.TESL
Lecturer and Examiner in
English and Education

"Business is a serious matter. Business travel can be a nuisance. How can associating the two be "fun"? Related with exceptional humor, Robert Naggar's travel experiences are a real eye opener on character study and on the supreme importance of human relations in business dealings. Highly enriching and excellent reading".

Mohamed Bendary
PEARL TRAVEL Director, Egypt.

DEDICATION

To Marion and Philip

"One's destination is never a place but a new way of seeing things."

Henry Miller

"We live in a wonderful world that is full of beauty, charm and adventure. There is no end to the adventures we can have if only we seek them with our eyes open."

Jawaharlal Nehru

My heartfelt thanks and gratitude to Annie and to Dr. Patricia Ross at Hugo House Publishers, Ltd. for their unfailing patience, advice and assistance.

CONTENTS

INTRODUCTION xi

CHAPTER 1: TAXI STORIES 17
- An amazing coincidence
- Back to the old mule
- Keep cool!
- Swiss police or Neapolitan police?

CHAPTER 2: CULTURAL GAPS 33
- Doktor Muller and mister Mike
- A meeting in Buenos-Aires
- Hans and Gretel in Swiss army land
- Annette, Ginette and Ludwig
- Twelve aasters?
- Where the Swiss match up to the French at the cheating game

CHAPTER 3: CHARACTERS 61
- The food buff
- The traveling saint
- The sex maniac

CHAPTER 4: EXPLOSIVE MIXTURES . . . 71
- Rough trip for Herbert
- Enough is enough!
- Looking for trouble
- Meeting the assassins

CHAPTER 5: NAPLES PARADISE OF . . . 101
BUSINESS ADVENTURERS
- First time in Naples
- Werner's discovery of life
- Raindrops from clear skies
- His lordship's bus trip back to town

CHAPTER 6: TWO LADIES 127
- A rough life
- A happy day to you

CONCLUSION 133

INTRODUCTION

"Son, what would you like to do for a living?"

The question came up time and again during my last year at high school. First it was father, then it was mother, then it was both at lunch or dinner, on school days, weekends, and even holidays. It became more and more pressing. No respite. No break. No escaping. I was cornered...understandably!

We were living in Africa, and my parents had to secure a place for me in a British university. I wasn't particularly gifted at anything, nor did I have an unshakeable ambition to become a doctor, lawyer or nuclear physicist, careers which would, at the time, according to my seniors, secure my future. Literature, music or fine arts were not subjects for discussion. These options were not considered serious and my dad repeatedly stated that he had no wish to finance a penniless, starving child to the end of his days.

These were times when there was practically no television and films were mainly American. Journalism was not a career, and nobody quite knew the real meaning of words such as "advertising and promotion." Computers, the Internet and mobile phones had yet to be invented. For those without a family trade or an established business, the selection of a university degree leading to a financially rewarding career was hence a serious problem.

"So, have you decided what you want to do or shall we decide for you?"

"I've decided: I want to travel."

"Travel is not a career. Do you want to become a sailor or a ship's captain?"

"Certainly not. I get seasick on a dinghy."

"All right then, your future is sealed. You'll become an engineer."

Those were also times when children didn't argue with parents. I thus became a graduate engineer and started work in a refrigerator factory. My grandiose engineering career ended in less than a year. I loathed to distraction a job which confined me to a production plant.

At that time, American multinationals were conquering Europe and, long before European companies, had well understood the need for face-to-face sales talks with their prospective or existing customers. They were recruiting young graduates by the bucket-load, and I was drafted as a marketing executive in a large corporation based in Geneva, Switzerland.

From then on, did I travel! Probably more than several trips to the moon and back and certainly more than in my wildest dreams. I first covered Europe, then, as my responsibilities evolved, the rest of the world.

In early junior positions, I usually boarded a flight on Monday evening, after the marketing group's motivation session, and returned on Thursday night, ready for the Friday morning's weekly review. This was tiring but exhilarating. These fast and recurring journeys were beyond my elderly father's comprehension:

"How can you live this way? Aren't you exhausted? Don't your American bosses have any consideration for your health? Isn't it dangerous to drive in all these foreign places?"

"Dad, my dream was to travel and that's exactly what I'm doing. I love every moment of it and wouldn't change my job for a millionaire's idle life! I meet fantastic people, there isn't a day when I don't see something new, wrestle with a new language, eat food I've never had before. What more could I ask for? I'm discovering the world!"

He just shook his head.

"I just can't believe it! This modern life is crazy!"

There was no explaining. Travel, whatever its reason, is an art and a pleasure. It is about meeting new folks, immersing oneself in new cultures, understanding how to get people, wherever they may be, to smile, to laugh, to listen not only to one's words but also to one's entire "being" and doing the same in return. Travel can foster a grand love of life and of humanity, wherever one goes, whatever one does.

For me, the sales objectives of my trips slowly became secondary to the importance of what I was able to discover. I noticed however, that, in the process, my professional performance increased beyond expectations, and my stature among my peers and within the company, progressively took another dimension.

I found that, when approached with an amiable smile, with a kind word and a listening ear, people were fundamentally friendly. The most irate taxi driver could often be turned into a smiling, chatty partner who poured all his pains onto you in an effort to release his tensions.

Travel is one of the best schools in the world to study psychology, sociology, and probably most all other "ologies" associated with human beings because, if you know how to listen, they will enrich you with their own life experience.

If you go to it with an open mind and a sense of humor, you will find not only fun, but endless wisdom worthy of the best philosophers.

What follows are some of my happenings as I traveled the world. I place it within the context of business only because that is the reason why I was able to experience so much. As such, this is not a travel guide, but rather the way to find fascination and beauty offered by the variety of humanity in these chance encounters.

Since those early days, travel habits have changed, the media has invaded our lives, things move faster, air safety regulations sometimes make us miserable, but I still travel often and always with joy, waiting for the next unexpected surprise to pop up from nowhere.

I hope what I relate here inspires my readers to travel to faraway places and have their own adventures. But be they far or close to home, may your trips always be cheerful, lucky and humanly enriching.

CHAPTER 1

TAXI STORIES

If avenues and roads are the arteries and veins of towns, then taxis are their blood, and taxi drivers reflect their life and soul.

In general, taxi drivers detest their work. In Europe, many of them are mature men who have lost their jobs and couldn't find another position in their profession. Others may be immigrants whose only skill is to drive a car. For many of them, driving a taxi is a last resort, an occupation they took up, too proud to beg for social aid.

Driving a taxi is an exhausting and ungrateful job. You are sitting all day either alert to the traffic or waiting for a client to hop into your own private space and who just gives you an address with no further exchange. There is no real appeal to this boring work and taxi drivers are often grumpy, sullen and silent unless... unless one can engage in a conversation which might kindle their interest, lighten their burden, and open their heart. This is often easy, sometimes difficult, but always rewarding.

In my travels, I fell upon historians, philosophers, literature buffs and, even once, on a qualified zoologist who told me more about baboons than I could ever imagine possible!

Excepting a language barrier, a seasoned taxi driver can transmit more intimate feelings about his town than could any opinionated politician. He is part of the city and senses its pulse, its vibrations, its heart.

Some of my most memorable encounters have been the chance happenings in a taxi, and to recount them here reminds me of the range of human emotion you can run across in one chance encounter.

AN AMAZING COINCIDENCE

The place is New York, Kennedy Airport in the late '70's.

I have just got off the Swissair flight from Geneva and am ready to rush to my hotel for a refreshing shower.

The terminal is as busy as an anthill, hot and humid with throngs of people desperate to find their luggage which they then wearily drag behind them as they lumber out of the building.

A long queue stretches as its line of tired travellers at the limo rank push and shove, trying to keep their place in the unruly crowd. I finally make it to the first row and, as usual with just a small suitcase, am the first in the car. After checking that their many bags have been loaded, three other passengers come on board and promptly collapse in their seats with a deep sigh of relief. The air conditioning revives us enough to dare a quick look at our fellow travellers. Friendly smiles are exchanged and we slowly relax as the limo leaves the airport. I am by far the youngest passenger. The others are in their late sixties or more, elderly people, as seen through my thirty year old eyes! The Afro-American driver is a jolly white haired character with a wide happy grin on his face.

We give him our respective destinations, all well-known hotels in Manhattan.

There is a lull as the limo speeds towards New-York but I sense an exchange of puzzled and quizzical looks between my fellow passengers. The gentleman sitting next to me looks more intently at the older man opposite him:

"Excuse me sir, could we have already met? Your face is familiar although I can't remember where I may have seen you before. My name is John D..... I am a lawyer."

"John D..., John D...! Yes, the name rings a bell. Were you by any chance involved in the anti-communist trials in New York in the 50's?"

"No, I was still in Germany then."

"Germany! Ah! That's the answer. I was a Judge at the Nuremberg trials after the war. My name is David R..... That's where we may have met."

"Yes! No doubt! I was one of the younger members of the Nazis prosecuting team."

"I now remember," says the judge who then starts recalling old memories.

"Hum, excuse me gentlemen, says the third passenger during a short silence, my name is Harry C.... I was a young reporter at NBC at the time and covered the trials for the station. It was indeed a fascinating period."

The atmosphere in the taxi is now warm and friendly as my travel companions exchange a wealth of memories and exciting stories about life in Germany in the late 40's.

As we get closer to our destinations, the three old friends exchange addresses and telephone numbers and pledge to get together again around a dinner table. The limo stops in front of a hotel. First to get off, the judge extracts his wallet from his pocket and holds out a ten dollar bill to the driver who turns round and faces us with a warm smile, his white teeth gleaming and his eyes shining with what appear to be tears of emotion:

"Hey Your Honour! You don't owe me nothin' Mister Judge! It's a pleasure to drive you around and this ride is on me! I am Sam F..., the mechanic who serviced and cleaned your Packard and who sold you four tyres on the black market when yours were as bald as a baby's buttocks. Enjoy your stay in New-York Mister Judge! Here's my phone number in case you need to get around."

A stunned silence of amazement was followed by an explosion of loud cheers, of laughter and of emotional embraces. People stopped in their tracks to look in bewilderment at the unusual scene of an impeccably dressed, distinguished gentleman hugging a shabby-looking old taxi driver, both of them in tears, clinging to one another as if anticipating the end of time!

Cars honked and impatient, busy pedestrians, slowed by the gathering crowd, started to protest. We had to move. The driver got back behind his wheel still heaving with emotion and, shaking his head in bewilderment, muttered to himself:

"Amazin'! Amazin'! Ain't this life just amazin'!"

BACK TO THE OLD MULE

Bilbao, Spain.

In those happy days without the Internet, we were still able to work like gentlemen, away from unwanted office calls. Sometimes, we also had to use our imagination to cope with unexpected situations.

That day, I had a morning meeting with Bill, the British-born manager of a Spanish company. Miles out of town, the factory was the first and only building of a new industrial development area. The land had probably been given to the company free of charge with no taxation on profits for many years since nobody in his right mind except a stingy accountant would have put a factory in that forsaken place. All around it were bucolic fields and the place only had two telephone lines to connect it to the outside world through its ancient phones and wheezy telex machines.

After a thirty kilometre drive out of Bilbao on secondary roads, the only access to it was through an atrociously bumpy un-surfaced country lane full of pot holes and covered with cowpats and mud.

No travelling salesman in his right mind would have wanted to visit the place more than once in his lifetime, but I happen to like the wilderness so went to see Bill three times a year. He always greeted me with enthusiasm and treated me to an excellent lunch before the friendly conclusion of a good contract with little bargaining. I always got to the place by taxi, a two hour drive from my hotel in Bilbao.

On that particular day, the sky was cloudless, the fields a tender green and I was engaged in a wide-ranging exchange of views on the state of the world with the driver.

Half an hour later, we ground to a halt with a flat tire. The ancient Seat had bumped into a pothole which had left a deep gash in the rubber. We stopped, changed the wheel and were off again…nothing unusual in this situation except that the philosophical exchange on the state of the world changed to swearing and railing against the government and local authorities for bad road maintenance.

The driver was a little grumpy and much more sober and subdued with his accelerator. Instead of gunning straight ahead like the ancient Conquistadores, he was now swerving carefully from side to side on the narrow road, trying intently, with an apologetic smile, to avoid the murderous potholes.

We could clearly see the holes but were not watchful of nails…and it was a big fat iron stud which, a few miles later, flattened a second tire. There was no other spare wheel and we were still far from the factory with no passing cars to help us out of our predicament.

The swearing and imprecating got louder. Cursing the government slowly shifted to blaming me, who could have no possible good reason for going to that godforsaken place. I was bringing him bad luck and thought I had better collect my suitcase and start walking, because Pedro wasn't inclined to go one inch further on that track. But Spaniards are kind people, so after crying a little over his bad luck, the man got back into his taxi and, very slowly and carefully started to drive along.

There were no distress lights on the old cab, so he waved his arm forlornly, holding a white handkerchief to signal his need for assistance but nothing came our way.

We were moving slowly at a snail's pace with three round wheels and an oval one…trolum…trolum… trolum, at five miles an hour, in total silence, for fear of scaring the two remaining tires. The gods, that day, had decided to have fun at our expense! Maybe Pedro had something to expiate or Moses had it against me, because the car was ever so slowly but surely, leaning more and more towards the right, when lo and behold, a third tyre went flat! There was no escaping our fate, we had to stop.

Like the genie in Aladdin's lamp, Pedro had given up swearing and become a subdued image of himself, resignedly muttering prayers to the taxi drivers' protective saints, begging for their kind assistance in his time of need.

His prayers were heard: the taxi driver's gods sent us a helping hand in the form of an old mule pulling an antique cart, driven by an ancient peasant who, seeing two distressed travellers humbly hunched up on the side of the road, stopped with a profusion of Arrr…Arrr!

To Pedro and me, Alfonso, his cart and his mule seemed like Cinderella's coach pulled by four white stallions. After considerable philosophical discussions on the subjects of growing wheat and on the hard times for farmers, the man declared himself ready to take us to the factory.

If, dressed in your grey flannel suit, you have never made your entrée in the forecourt of a company, sitting on the floor of a mule-driven cart, you have missed something important in your life! Everybody from the gate keeper to the highest company official runs out to welcome you, making sure that you are all right! You are fêted, pampered, offered rum, gin, wine, coffee, tea or whatever you wish, to alleviate your distress.

Disgruntled and wretched on arrival to the factory, my friend Pedro, highly impressed by the welcome we received, embraced me as if, brothers in arms, we had conquered the world. For a soccer-loving Spaniard, he now felt part of a great winning team and, in a way, we were. We had overcome a predicament, though small as it seems now, appeared insurmountable at the time.

The company manager who, although always very friendly, had considered me a mere "travelling salesman," now regarded me as a man of courage and superb moral strength, worthy of respect and consideration.

From then on, every time I made an appointment to see Bill, a shiny company car came to fetch me in Bilbao and, after my meeting, drove me back to my hotel. There was less haggling than ever before over our deals, and Bill remained my faithful customer. But I must say, after our intrepid adventure on the mule cart, the shiny car never compared!

———

KEEP COOL!

The place is Taipei.

The evening traffic is heavy and I am sitting in a taxi returning to the hotel.

The driver is a highly strung young man who has probably been driving for twelve hours or more and appears ready to murder anybody who gets in his way.

I am a little tense myself, watching him swerve crazily in and out of lanes, accelerating fiercely to gain one place in the crawling queue, then braking like a maniac to avoid bumping into the car in front.

With what I hope looks like a serene and relaxed smile, I try to speak to the young man, suggesting that I am in no hurry and that I will pay him a good tip if he relaxes and drives a little slower. Alas, I quickly realise that he couldn't care less about the comfort of his good-for-nothing client sitting at the back of his cab.

As an answer and to assert his rights, he shakes his fist and swears at other drivers with words which appear, at best, to mean that they should be at home putting nappies to their babies!

At one point, a man ahead of us, as aggressive as my driver and determined not to let us pass, swerves and matches every one of our crazy zigzags.

My young friend is getting more and more irate, screams like a mad baboon, shakes his fist and wishes the driver in front to burn in hell for all eternity!

Traffic stops at a traffic light. Our tormentor is two cars ahead in the line next to ours. I thank the Lord for having heard my prayer and given me a few seconds' respite. But to my alarm, my driver bends forwards, pulls out a lethal-looking pointed metal bar from under his seat, flings open his door, jumps out of the taxi, and races to his enemy's car. Quick as lightning and before the other driver has even seen him, he frantically and repeatedly knives the two back tyres of the stopped car.

He then races back to our taxi, just in time to tear off as the traffic lights turn green.

He quickly hides the metal bar back under his seat then looks at the scene behind us in his rear mirror and starts shaking with uncontrollable laughter. I turn round and see our hapless enemy running after us like a demon, shaking his fists crazily and swearing like trouper. Stopped in the middle of the traffic, his car blocks everybody and, oblivious to his sorrows, the other drivers hoot impatiently and swear at him. Except for the inexcusable violence, the scene looks like an extract from a crazy cartoon. I am ashamed to admit that, although a little shaken, I laugh too, praying there will be no red traffic light to stop us.

Now rid of his pent up frustration, my driver rocks with laughter, imitating his enemy's helpless fist-shaking in the midst of the honking cars.

Due to a language barrier impossible to bridge, I clearly couldn't have altered this young man's aggressive temper. However, after his highly reprehensible deed at the expense of his opponent, his fit of rage overcome, he slowly returned to his amiable self. Sometimes, when it comes to uncontrolled anger, not interfering may be the better option.

When we reached the hotel, I paid him his fare and we smiled at each other, unexpected partners in an unusual, if objectionable, character scene.

SWISS POLICE OR NEAPOLITAN POLICE?

It is 11 o'clock on a dark winter night.

I am on a tedious flee-jump flight from Geneva to Naples with three stops in between. The weather is dreadful. After every take-off and before every landing, we dance like drunken yoyos in the middle of vicious thunderstorms. As black clouds and screaming winds cross borders between one country and another, they don't adapt their fury to the often gentle characters of the people who inhabit the territories they traverse! Whether over Switzerland, France or Italy, thunderstorms are just as foul and violent tempered as one another!

I abhor thunderstorms when flying ever since an old Fokker turboprop I was in some years earlier, was twice hit by lightning which blew up the controls of its landing gear. This forced the pilot to circle above the nearest available airport while, below us, frantic fire brigades with psychedelic flash-lights and screaming sirens, generously spread foam on the runway awash with rain and hailstones as big as hens' eggs. It was most heart-lifting and entertaining to watch ambulances line up along the runway as our crippled aircraft, flying at low altitude, was bombarded by hail as if assaulted by machine guns fired by thousands of merciless guerrilla fighters... but I'm still alive and that's another story.

On that particular winter night, as many times before, I wished I were back home, cosily huddled in front of a warm fire instead of being bounced about like a rubber ball in a dingy cylindrical rat-trap!

To forget my misery, I was trying to concentrate on the drivel I was reading in a Swiss newspaper where a story finally caught my attention. It was so utterly absurd and so typically Swiss that it was hard to believe.

Switzerland is an unusual country. Its larger neighbors, France, Italy and Germany are fairly monolithic republics each with a single national language and education system and with laws which apply over the entire country. Switzerland, whose total population is smaller than that of New-York, consists of twenty six fiercely independent-minded regions, the Cantons, each with its own government which holds wide powers in its own small fiefdom. The country has four official languages and as many education systems and police forces as there are Cantons!

Although the forces of law and order closely cooperate, police from one Canton has no right of action in another even when pursuing a confirmed bandit. Needless to say, the different police forces are well-organised, rather ticklish on rules and regulations, and very uptight on their local prerogatives.

The story I was reading related that the police of Canton Bern was hot on the trail of a criminal who had committed a major robbery in a well-known jewellery store of the country's capital. The robbing of jewellery is something which the average Swiss consider worse than an act of high treason. Indeed, the industry contributes generously to the national and local taxation revenues, and in Switzerland, one does not joke with money, especially when it concerns the citizens' taxes. The thief had been seen tearing off in a green Volkswagen whose number had been recorded and all forces in the country were alerted and on the lookout, ready to pounce on this heinous enemy of the people.

Sometime on that same afternoon the Bernese police headquarters were called by their colleagues of the neighbouring Canton Aargau. The gangster had been caught in their region and was currently detained in Aargau's prison. Would the kind colleagues from Bern come and collect the unpleasant individual.

Two Bernese cops promptly jumped in an unmarked car and rushed to Aargau. They got to the local police HQ, collected their handcuffed prisoner, signed the discharge papers and took off like lightening back to Bern.

The speed limit on the Swiss motorways is one hundred and twenty kilometres per hour but our friends were in much of a hurry to get home for dinner and drove like bats out of hell at one hundred and eighty kilometres per hour. The fines for speeding are extremely stiff in the country and, if a driver is caught at thirty kilometres over the speed limit, his license can be withdrawn on the spot and his car confiscated. The way in which he then proceeds with his trip does not concern the police; he can walk back home for all they care!

As our Bernese Police friends were speeding down the motorway in their unmarked car, an Aargau police vehicle appeared behind them and signalled them to stop.

Confident and serene in their own good right since they were acting in the course of duty, the Bernese duly stopped and explained the situation to their Aargau colleagues. These did not see the situation in the same light and took their time to record a full statement and to notify the Bernese that they were needlessly driving at a reckless speed, endangering other motorists' lives.

Their first impulse was also, no doubt, to confiscate their colleague's driving license but, since this could leave them with the headache of dealing with the villain sitting at the back of the offending vehicle, they settled for a heavy fine to the impetuous driver who had no alternative but to comply with the law and pay up there and then.

During the whole complex and lengthy process, the handcuffed thief, a foreigner to the country, no doubt laughed his head off at the absurdities of the Swiss police forces.

Picturing the scene, I thoroughly enjoyed the story which was a delight of Swiss culture, civic sense and spirit of local independence over central government's arrogance and invasion of regional prerogatives.

At long last, we landed in Naples in the thick of night, in gale-force wind and heavy rain.

The hotel was far from the airport so I jumped in the first available taxi, relishing in advance a hot bath and a well-deserved rest.

Naples is a very special place and, further in this book, a whole chapter is devoted to its inhabitants' fantasies.

Enough at this stage to say that Neapolitans rarely observe traffic regulations. To the average local citizen, traffic signals simply do not exist and each driver follows his own ways and fancies, intent only on avoiding trouble to himself and his car.

Scarcely waiting for me to shut the door, the taxi driver took off as if Satan himself with a cohort of fiendish devils were after him. Sitting at the back of the car, I was jogged about like a dismembered puppet. The road was slippery and the occasional fierce slamming of breaks sent us wildly skidding on its surface.

Like any other Neapolitan driver, my cabby happily ignored red traffic lights, his two feet dancing an unrhythmical samba between the accelerator and the brake pedals.

If you ask a mad driver in Naples to slow down, he is likely to get highly offended and either drive even faster to prove his talent, or stop on the spot and ask you to leave his cab, abandoning you to your fate. In this foul weather, the risk was not worth taking so, a little tired of being taken for a plastic ball in a baby's rattle and trying to distract him from his Formula One racing act, I attempted a friendly conversation, commenting on the bad weather and the rough road. My neighbourly approach did not seem to have much effect on Speedy Gonzalez so, trying another tack, I played the ignorant foreigner. We had just passed four red traffic lights at full speed so I asked him why taxi drivers in Naples didn't obey traffic signals.

His reply was that only cowards and foreigners stopped at traffic lights and that I should take no notice of them since most of them served no purpose whatsoever!

While he was educating me on Neapolitan driving customs, the cyclical blue glare of a police car's flashlight invaded the taxi. I turned round to see that the police, although right behind us, did not seem to chase us but, rather oblivious to our repeated traffic offences, was in a hurry to overtake us.

Possibly shaken by the concomitance of our conversation and of the sudden appearance of the police, my driver stepped hard on the breaks and stopped at the next red traffic lights....and bang! Avoiding a head-on collision with the oncoming traffic, the police car crashed straight into us. Our cab bounced five yards ahead and I was catapulted head over heels over the front seat. Seconds after the shock, oblivious to my uncomfortable position, my driver started screaming and swearing at the top of his voice. He jumped out of the car and, gesticulating as only Italians know how, ran up and down the road in the middle of speeding traffic, calling every living mortal around as a witness against these accursed foreigners and good for nothing police drivers.

I finally made it to my feet and got out to look at the damage: the taxi was three feet shorter and the police's Alfa Romeo, its front deeply embedded in the boot of the cab, was oozing water in every direction.

Standing next to me, the police driver was shaking his head, his face contorted with rage. He walked up to my driver to whom, as a start and in cold fury, he delivered an almighty clout in the face, then shouted at him in local dialect:

"You cretin, you idiot, you driver of my ass' backside, you good for nothing son of a whore, why did you stop?"

"But the traffic light was red, answered my driver looking at me murderously, and my passenger asked me to stop."

"So what, you moron!" replied the policeman. "You did not stop at any of the previous red traffic lights, why did you stop at this particular one? And anyway, you should not listen to your passengers' advice especially if they are foreigners! Just drive like a Neapolitan, you half-witted mule! Now get your car out of the way and show me your papers."

I tried to intervene in favour of my hapless driver who was, I thought, unfairly treated, and confirmed that I had indeed asked him to stop at red traffic lights. The policeman, very amiably answered with a smile of pity at my simple-mindedness:

"Do excuse us sir, you have really been unlucky. A Neapolitan taxi driver should drive like a Neapolitan. We understand that you come from another country where customs may be different but here, people should not follow one rule one moment then another just because somebody asks them to. Your driver never stopped at any traffic light and should therefore not have stopped at this last one. He is unreliable, irresponsible and dangerous. For your own safety, we will get a police car to drive you to your hotel!"

Indeed his colleague had already called the nearest station and a second police car, all sirens screaming, was arriving at great speed.

Despite my taxi driver's lamentable wails, it was evident he would not win his plea, would be accused of reckless driving, probably be heavily fined, and left to pay for his own damages.

As I got into the shiny official Alfa Romeo, I left him in tears of rage, swearing at me and vowing revenge. Naples being a place where a man's honour is valued above his life, I wondered whether I would ever dare to step out of the hotel and ever get back to Switzerland alive.

I sat as quiet as a mouse at the back of the speeding police car. Its driver, of course, ignored all traffic lights, cross roads, one way streets and other such useless oddities and brought me to my hotel in three minutes, after crossing town like a rocket at about one hundred miles per hour!

When we stopped, my teeth were chattering, my knees were weak, my stomach thoroughly upset. The driver once again apologized for my taxi driver's ineptitude and assured me that they would submit him to a new driving test just to teach him a lesson.

With this, he wished me a good stay in Naples and tore off leaving half of his tires' treads on the tarmac.

At last in my hot bath, I wondered - but only for a moment - which I preferred: The dependable, strict and predictable but humourless Swiss police or the anarchic, extravagant and unpredictable Neapolitan drivers, full of unexpected fantasy and exotic charm.

CHAPTER 2

CULTURAL GAPS

Each step of a trip in a foreign land can either be the beginning of a grand adventure or can lead to anybody's downfall. Problems may be caused by cultural differences, language barriers, physical demeanour or just simple habits.

The examples of light blunders or unintentional offence are infinite and will, in general, result in a good laugh with a friendly pat on the back. Some innocent mistakes can be more unpleasant and call for a sheepish grin and profuse apology; others may lead to more serious consequences.

Whatever the case, these slip-ups will be interesting lessons, inducing us to see the world through different lenses. They will enrich and widen our personal experience and open our minds to the better understanding and acceptance of other cultures.

―――

DOKTOR MULLER AND MISTER MIKE

The place is Frankfurt-Germany.

Our large multinational company had just announced a fantastic new product which would make all other pharmaceuticals look like pills for sneezing rats. This one had it all: anti-allergic, anti-fat, anti-depression, anti-conception and anti-every-virus ever to be born on the face of this earth! To top it all, it could be made a pleasing pink for fair ladies or dark blue for serious executives!

I had been involved in long and complex negotiations with a large conservative German company, a model of Teutonic organisation and efficiency, which offered to act as exclusive distributor of the miracle product in Europe. Discussions had been protracted. We, of course, wanted a million-dollar-a-minute for our new wonder baby and submitted a proposal which tied the Germans hands, knees, tongues and eyelids. They, in turn, offered a counter-proposal in the form of a thousand page document written in ancient Bavarian which, in our company, nobody could or was interested to read, it being nothing but a usual business transaction in its early stages!

After months of haggling, we had finally reached a point where "the big boys" could, at long last, meet for a reasonably friendly and possibly conclusive chat. "We" lowly mortals, had invested many countless hours of "dirty work", sadly munching through tasteless sandwiches and drinking soda or plain water during our working lunches. "They" could now get together for supper at Maxim's with caviar, champagne and dancing girls, grant interviews to the press then just sit back and relax while congratulating one another on the great job "they" had done... nothing but the usual day's work!

The German company's top management consisted of stern and very formal elderly gentlemen whose sense of humour during our many meetings, had proved as developed as that of a grizzly bear disturbed by a dancing racoon during its winter sleep. Even after several weeks of negotiations, a meeting in their boardroom invariably started with our usual team of three standing in line at the room's entrance door while their eight managers involved in the discussions filed in one by one in military order for the formal handshake session. As one of them stepped in front of one of us, he looked straight into our eyes, grabbed hold of our hand, gripped it in a vice, crushing the bones to a pulp, then clicked his heels, lowered his head in a swift movement and clearly announced his surname while dismembering our arm with a vigorous handshake. He then stepped sideways and started the same act all over again with the next one of us down the line.

The President, Herr Doktor Muller, was about seventy, six foot tall with a white mane, a strong chin and a no-nonsense air about him which prevented even minimal attempts at amicable small-talk.

To finalize the contract, our company had delegated an American fast-track yuppie business team typical of the business climate of the eighties. Its leader, Michael Applesby, was a boisterous and slap-happy whizz-kid in his late thirties with a superb brain for money-spinning business deals but very limited international experience. His team of three young, hard-working and hard-playing members consisted of a lawyer and two technical specialists.

It was Mike's first trip to Germany and before coming he had warned me that he was as curious as a mouse and wanted to see everything, try everything and do anything he could not do in his native provincial North Carolina town.

Two hours after landing from his long flight, Mike was ready for shopping. The first windows which attracted him like magnets were those of Beate Uhse's and Doktor Muller's sex shops. These are today an integral part of every respectable shopping area in Germany, but at the time, they were still relatively new. Mike had never seen anything like this. Once he had stepped in the first sex shop, we could not pull him away from the "Mickey Mouse" condoms, the inflatable naked ladies, the mechanical and electrical gadgets meant to instantaneously transform faithful wives and shy children-loving mothers into sex-demented Aphrodites who would, in a flash, turn their unsuspecting hard-working and tranquil husbands into exhausted and defeated stallions!

Mike's curiosity was insatiable, and had it not been for his hungry colleagues, he would have skipped his meals to read the technical notices and there and then try out some of the gadgets he had bought. While he was raving at the gimmicks, his lawyer was tearing his hair out, imagining the disaster that would occur if a customs officer opened his suitcase and discovered its contents.

Our first evening was devoted to wild imagination and fantasy about the ways our young team-leader would set the world on fire in North Carolina. The following morning, Mike came down to breakfast with battered eyes but with a happy heart! After coffee, eggs and bacon, he was ready to finalize the biggest contract in his short but so- far successful business life.

The taxi dropped us in front of the German firm's imposing headquarters. We announced ourselves to the flawlessly groomed hostess at the entrance desk and were escorted to the magnificent board room where the table was laid with leather-bound blocks of paper and silver pens, all embossed in golden letters to the Company's name. Mike walked straight in and sat down in one of the luscious armchairs, ready to take command of the meeting.

At the first stroke of nine on the grandfather clock, Herr Doktor Muller and his many assistants filed in. Mike jumped to attention and the hand-shaking introduction session started. It ended only when all the titles and detailed responsibilities of each member of both delegations had been given out *in extenso*.

Herr Doktor Muller imperiously assigned a seat to each of us and we all stood behind our respective armchairs, waiting for his cue to be seated so that business could commence.

For Mike, this long ceremony was a little too formal. He thought that the best way to release the Teutonic tension induced by the stern Doktor Muller and stamp it with his own style was to crack a joke.

As we all sat down, he declared in his warm brawl:

"Hey Doktor, I found out last night that you had already implemented a great idea! I guess *you* could give us some good tips on fancy and successful new products rather than the other way round!"

A great silence followed while everybody wondered what Mike was referring to then, with his pronounced German accent, Herr Doktor Muller ponderously asked:

"Ideas? Vat ideas is dat Herr Applesby?"

"Hell! You should know Doktor! These great sex shops of yours! They're all over town!"

A deadly hush settled in the room. The German team did not quite understand what the young American meant.

"Shops? Vat are deeze shops Mr. Appelsby, I do not understand your meaning."

"Hey Doktor! You should know! The Doktor Muller sex shops! You know! Ha Ha! Great idea! They will make us all millionaires!"

There was a gasp; all heads turned towards Herr Doktor Muller. The old gentleman turned pale, clearly out of his depth. After a few seconds that lasted an eternity, he placed both his hands flat on the table, stood up straight as a ramrod, nodded briefly at nobody in particular then martially walked out without uttering a single word. The German team got up as one man and marched out after him in deadly silence, looking straight ahead without a single glance in our direction to say good bye.

Mike stood up in alarm.

"Hey! What did I say? I was only joking! Hey gentlemen, I didn't mean to ...."

But there was no longer anybody there to hear him; they were all gone, leaving the door wide open for us to leave!

Mike was aghast, speechless, uncomprehending, shaking his head in wonder.

"I'll be damned! You can't even crack an innocent joke with these guys! Can't they understand that I didn't mean it seriously? Come on Bob, bring them back! Tell them I'm stupid, tell them anything but for Heaven's sake bring them back in here!"

I looked at Mike then at my other colleagues. The twinkle in their eyes and their barely suppressed ironic smiles were too much to take. Except for our dismayed team leader whose downfallen expression said it all, we exploded into uncontrollable laughter, tears pouring from our eyes. Done, finished, gone! *Aufwiedersehen* the contract of the century, the cooperation, the fortune to be made, the months of painful efforts... all gone up in smoke because of a silly wisecrack!

As far as I know, Mike did not return to Europe for our company and he certainly became much more careful with his jokes during meetings.

This business failure, to which, unfortunate as it was, all actors happily survived, is a stark reminder of several important human factors when encountering people even in one's own country. These may be, amongst other, age difference, upbringing, and knowledge of historical changes in the person's country during his or her life. In this particular case, the political transformation in Germany had been dramatic.

Doktor Muller had lived through the Nazi period and had possibly been himself involved in this hideous regime. Although now living in a highly democratic society, his personal comportment and culture appeared to have evolved little since those dark years. The mere mention of "sex" was so repulsive to him that it wiped out all other considerations. He and his company would not, under any circumstance, deal with people who brought the topic, even in jest, in a meeting room. Mike, the young and happy American, had been totally oblivious to Dr. Muller's background and culture, clearly shown, from the very beginning of the meeting, by the director's quasi military attitude.

One overarching benefit of travel, if you're observant, is that you can look at life through the eyes of the person you are speaking to, rather than through your own. Just observing the person move, sit, smile, his or her facial movements, the twinkle or lack of it in his or her eyes, or listening to the way he or she greets you, will allow you to quickly shed your own skin and clothe yourself in his or hers'. Being able to do this can not only save large business deals, but also vastly enrich one's life.

———

A MEETING IN BUENOS-AIRES

This last story reminds me of another event which took place some years ago. It happened in Buenos Aires, in the large conference room of the high tower of the Telecommunication Building overlooking Rio de Plata, the river which flows through the city. The occasion was a decisive meeting related to a multi-million dollar tender to be awarded by the Argentinean company.

The reunion was the last of a harassing day both for the buying team and for the prospective suppliers. I was accompanied by our company's lawyer and technical director. The Argentinean delegation was headed by the corporation's purchasing director, a relatively gruff middle-aged lady with a closed, sullen face, handsomely dressed and with beautiful blue eyes. She had already been through three of these meetings with our competitors, was obviously tired and fed-up with the whole affair, and probably ready to dismiss us at our slightest blunder.

While a legal discussion was raging over some minor terms of the contract, I turned round to look at the Rio de Plata. The sun was a perfectly round shining orange globe, slightly masked by a light haze, and was setting over the river. It was a dramatically beautiful sight, too gorgeous to miss. In a flash, I thought that the sullen Argentinean director might have been, some years earlier, a beautiful young woman who may have had a romantic moment in front of such a sight. She was then sitting at the conference table, shoulders hunched, with her back to the window.

"Excuse me gentlemen, could we please stop our discussion for a moment. We have something important happening right under our eyes which we cannot miss."

Under the surprised and disconcerted looks of all participants, I got up, went over to the director's seat, took the startled lady's hand, begged her to stand, and walked her, totally bewildered, to the large bay-window.

"Madam, we just cannot miss such beauty which is offered to us by Nature. Could we please take a few minutes' break to watch this amazing sunset?"

All participants got up and joined us at the window. The moment was magic. When we sat down to resume our talks, voices were hushed, people were different, the atmosphere had changed. The purchasing director was now sitting straight, her face serene and smiling.

"Gentlemen," she said, "I'd first like to thank Mr. Naggar for this interruption and for this beautiful moment. Are there really significant technical or legal differences between our corporation's needs and these gentlemen's offer?"

Both technical and legal specialists shook their heads in denial.

"Well then, I suggest we end this meeting and thank our guests for their efforts to comply with our requirements."

We all got up, shook hands with smiling faces, and quietly left the room in a totally different mood than when we had entered it.

I never got to know whether we had made the best technical offer or bid the lowest price, but we won the tender. For that, my company was very pleased.

The Argentinean Company's requirements were quite standard within our industry and, much like we did, our competitors no doubt answered them successfully.

My guess is that the beautiful sunset and the sweet moment of kinship which resulted may have made the difference.

HANS AND GRETEL IN SWISS ARMY LAND

The drive from Geneva to Hans' factory was a real pleasure. The plant was in one of the prettiest parts of Switzerland. The offices had large bay windows open on a breath-taking view of a lake surrounded by snow-capped mountains. People in the company were exquisitely amiable, business discussions were always friendly, price negotiations always fair and payments were made with the precision of a Swiss watch. This ideal customer made you wonder why all the world of business could not operate along the same easy and happy lines, making life simple and relaxing for everybody.

Hans' father had started his company some years earlier as a small subcontractor of micro-electronic boards. His workers were then mostly part-time employees of the surrounding rural community seeking an activity during winter months. He had thought of a farm-related security device and, with a team of college students, had developed an ingenious product for this particular niche market. His small family business had quickly become one of those industrial wonders often found in the valleys of Switzerland, a respected and successful worldwide leader in its specialized field of activity.

My relations with Hans and his family had become very friendly, a rare privilege for somebody who did not speak *Schweizerdeutsch*, was not a native Swiss and could neither yodel nor drink a full glass of home-made kirsch in one gulp, without flinching!

Hans' wife, Gretel, was a beautiful young woman of cheerful character and charming smile and their two children were models of politeness and good manners. After some years of friendly business relations, the family had insisted that, when I visited their company, I stay overnight at their house

Hans had three passions which sealed our friendship, ski, tennis, and chess. He beat me flat at the two sports, and I taught him a few tricks at the board game. After my arrival at their place in late afternoon, we would have supper then spend the evening squinting in deep concentration at our respective kings, queens, bishops and castles until our eyelids drooped. In the morning we would have a quick business discussion which resulted in the extension of an existing order or in the conclusion of a new contract. Then, depending on the season, we would spend the rest of the day either skiing or playing tennis.

A customer as reliable, solid and square as Hans is every salesman's dream, and there was no conceivable way one could expect an unconventional or unusual event to happen during a visit to his company.

It was time for contract renewal so I phoned for an appointment, relishing in advance the wonderful two days I would spend in the mountains.

Once a year, as most adult and able Swiss men, Hans dutifully performed his military service, sacrificing five weeks of his precious time to the army. As an officer, he devoted more than his fair share to the defence of his country, but took it good naturedly and saw this duty as a privilege rather than as the pain in the backside which many Swiss consider it to be.

I had seen a picture of Hans in uniform. His thick boots, rifle on the shoulder, heavy knapsack and aggressive moustache portrayed the image of a brutal, conquering Hun. The quiet and friendly man I knew who lived in a country which had known no conflict for over five hundred years, looked like a fierce fighter of a land at war, ready to lead the whole world to destruction.

Hans answered my call and informed me that, much to his regret, he could not see me during the following few weeks because he would be in the army. However precision being the essence of Switzerland, it was unthinkable for him to miss or postpone a contract renewal date so he invited me to come as usual and negotiate the new agreement with his father. He also told me that, true to our tradition, I was expected to stay overnight in his house and that he would be most offended if I refused.

I felt that the invitation went beyond the rules of friendly hospitality but my customer was so insistent about it that, not wishing to offend him, I gladly accepted and arrived, as planned, in the late afternoon of a cold November day.

Lights were ablaze in the house. Gretel welcomed me with her usual charming smile, the children thanked me for the traditional box of chocolates and, after supper, purring like contented cats, we sat in the lounge in front of a warm fire. No effort of conversation was needed. The television was on for whoever wanted to watch but, not understanding a word of *Schweizerdeutsch*, with the permission of Gretel, I buried myself in a book on life in rural Switzerland in the Middle-Ages.

Contrary to what it is today, Switzerland was then a very poor country where peasants had to toil like slaves for a meagre harvest, sleep on damp straw litters in unheated shacks and eat whatever they could lay their hands on ... a far cry from this house of warmth, opulence and deep sofas in which I was slowly dozing off. At half past eight, upon a gentle but firm glance from their mother, the children got up, disappeared for a few moments to change into their pyjamas and returned smelling of minted toothpaste and rose-scented soap. They kissed uncle Bob and Mummy good night and went off to their rooms.

Gretel commented:

"They are wonderful children. They usually make a fuss about going to bed except when their father is away in the army. They then go to their room without a murmur."

"Yes, I expect they are a little sad and miss his presence."

"Oh no," she said, "that is not the reason. When Hans is in the army, we sleep on the floor and they take this very seriously."

I wondered if I had heard correctly or whether perhaps Gretel"s command of English had not allowed her to express what she really meant. I questioned:

"Sleep on the floor? Why would they sleep on the floor when Hans is away?"

"That is not quite correct. When Hans travels on business, we sleep in our beds but when he is in the army, we sleep on the floor out of solidarity for his suffering. This, we feel, is our own contribution, if only in spirit, to the defence of our country."

Having myself spent some time, albeit very short, in Swiss army barracks, I knew that the "suffering" was very relative and that, at least in Geneva, distress was more related to the consequences of drinking binges than to hard military exertions.

"I suppose you put mattresses on the floor. The children must think it fun!"

"No, no!" answered Gretel, clearly shocked at my treating so lightly such a serious subject. "We sleep on the carpets but we do put a small cushion under our heads."

"You do that too, Gretel?" I asked in disbelief

"Yes, of course, we all do it out of solidarity," she insisted as if I were a little dumb. "Even our guests do it if they have no objection. It is all for the strengthening of bonds between Swiss citizens. Whether in the army or not, all able-bodied Swiss males must be ready to suffer hardship together and to be ready to unite fraternally in case of war. If you wish, I will show you to your room."

That was where, right next to a beckoning warm and comfortable bed, I saw a rough grey army blanket folded on the floor with a somewhat flat and mean-looking cushion next to it.

"Of course, you don't *have* to sleep on the floor if you don't want to," said Gretel with her warm smile, "but since you recently became Swiss yourself, I expect you may want to show your solidarity with your newly adopted fellow countrymen!"

She then sweetly wished me good night and left me to meditate on my patriotic feelings.

I was just defeated by the simple abnegation of this woman and by the spirit of kinship she induced in her family.

I forlornly changed into my pyjamas then sat on the bed, chin in my palms, back hunched, deep in thought at the misery and discomfort I would have to endure on the stone-like floor while Hans, the lucky devil, was probably comfortably sleeping in a snug lieutenant's bed, in deep and happy dreams, snoring his lazy night away!

Concrete floors are hard, even when carpeted. I woke up in morning all aches and pains, stiff as a steel rod and with a throbbing head. At breakfast, I hazily heard myself thanking Gretel for her wonderful idea and for the excellent sleep I'd had on the comfort of her carpet. I also insisted on the moral satisfaction it had given me to share the sacrifice of her dear husband and of all the Swiss conscripts put together.

Hans' father got the better of me on the contract negotiation and I made sure I never visited Hans' factory again during the hardships of his military service.

ANNETTE, GINETTE AND LUDWIG

The place is a four-star hotel off the Champs-Elysées in Paris.

I had been asked to introduce Ludwig, a colleague from another division of our company, to one of my French customers.

I did not know Ludwig other than for the fact of seeing him in the halls and cafeteria of the company. He was a tall, blond and handsome man from Munich in his early forties. I could extract no useful information about his professional skills but corridor whispers taught me that he was more than a little infatuated with himself and proud of his feats as a womaniser. A married man with two children, Ludwig had apparently had affairs with a few of our secretaries but none appeared to have lasted more than a few weeks.

Olga, a flirtatious young lady who had worked in the same group as Ludwig was now working with us. I could not resist the temptation of learning a little more about my future travel companion.

"Olga my dear, I'm travelling with Ludwig next week. What's he like?"

"He is as stupid as he's handsome. Don't try to explain anything to him. It's a waste of time. He's just dumb!"

Not a single further word came out of Olga's pretty lips. I thought that her dismissive statement was rather harsh and that she may have been a little upset by the handsome salesman so, by the time I boarded my plane with Ludwig, I had forgotten all about it.

En route, we, of course complained about our new director. That good-for-nothing newcomer from the American boondocks had decreed that, despite the huge profits made by the company, five-star hotels in Paris were a thing of the past and that all travelling personnel would have to settle for four-star shacks. That was indeed a fall from Heaven to Purgatory and we wondered where this despicable man would stop his stingy nonsense! "Four-stars" we agreed, were still acceptable but not quite the same as five. When you have been going to a "five-star" for a while and have generously tipped the receptionists, concierges and bell-boys, you are treated like a lord. As you walk in, you are conspicuously greeted by your name and ordinary customers stop and look, wondering in which "beautiful people" review they have already seen your face. It gives you, for a precious little moment, the illusion of being in the shoes of Richard Gere in *Pretty Woman* as he escorts Julia Roberts to their hotel on Sunset Boulevard. This, when you are in your early thirties, is a big thrill!

Ludwig had no experience of Paris hotels so, during supper, I informed him of some of the risks he should avoid.

At the time, one of the tricks of hotel prostitutes was to leave a small box of matchsticks at the door of the rooms occupied by single men. If the box was collected by the unsuspecting (or knowledgeable) client as he returned to his room for the night, he would, sometime later, hear a discreet little knock on his door. When he opened it, he would find a smiling lady eager to fulfil her duties. If she had several customers to service on the same floor, she would often save time by not re-dressing between jobs and present herself completely naked.

The reason I knew this, was that some weeks earlier I had innocently collected a matchbox from the floor in front of my door and, in good Swiss tradition of tidiness, had put it in the ashtray on the table in my room. I had then gone to bed with a good conscience and quickly fallen asleep. Later, I thought I heard a discreet scratching on the door followed by a knock, then another, then others again which increased in intensity as I slowly emerged from my slumber. Drowsily I got up, squinted at my watch and focusing with difficulty, saw that it was three in the morning. Dragging myself to the door, I opened it slowly, making sure the latch was on and stood there with blinking eyes, gaping stupidly at a smiling, stark naked woman perched on bright red high heeled shoes.

"Here I am for the little service," she said obligingly.

I answered that she had certainly got the wrong room and shut the door. A loud bang and a curse totally ended my drowsiness.

"My matchbox, I want my matchbox!"

The matchbox! After rummaging through my brain, I remembered picking one up and suddenly understood its obvious purpose. I fetched it from the tray, wrapped it in a one hundred Franc note to avoid further swearing, gave it to the kind lady through the latched door, and went back to finish my night's sleep. (I suspect my reader might not believe this but I promise it is true. This was still a time when French francs hadn't been replaced by Euros).

I was telling this story to Ludwig as a warning to be careful and not let himself be fooled by professional prostitutes' tricks, but he laughed it off, scoffing at how stupid a green-hatter like me could be!

After supper, we went back to the hotel and, as usual when travelling in pairs, went to the bar for a night-cap. There were, of course, many very proper-looking young women chatting with a drink on their table. Not being much of a drinker, I wished Ludwig good night and left him after a last warning of caution.

In the thick of night, I was woken by shrill voices coming from the room next door, followed by what sounded like someone being hit, loud protests, a door opened then banged shut, scuttling feet down the corridor then wailing calls from Ludwig:

"Bob! Help! Help!"

I jumped out of bed and rushed to Ludwig's door which was shut. I could hear the man inside crying in pain.

"Help, please help!"

I ran down the stairs, shook the night porter awake, explained that my next door neighbour called for assistance and was probably too sick to get up and open his door. Could he please come with his master-key?

Annoyed and grumbling, the man got to the lift, pressed the fourth-floor button, and walked down the corridor to the room where cries for help were coming from. He realized that something serious was happening and now completely awake, opened the door in a hurry. We both rushed in.

A sight from the worst "who-done-it" greeted us:

Ludwig lay stark naked, spread-eagled on the bed, his two hands and two feet solidly strapped to the brass bedposts. His face and torso were scratched and bleeding, the room was a total mess and his wallet lay open and empty on the table.

The porter looked at me with a smile of deep commiseration and contempt.

"Not very bright your friend ... and please sir, no scandal; keep it quiet for his own sake."

Upon which he left me to untie the poor Ludwig who clearly lived up to Olga's able assessment of him.

"But Bob I swear I only invited them in for a drink, then they suggested we had another... We had many drinks and a very interesting conversation. They were nice girls and we talked about Germany, Wagner and Goethe. They were very well educated. The bar was closing and they said they wished to have a last drink with me before leaving so I invited them to my room. After this last whisky, they suggested that we shouldn't finish such a nice evening without a good time. They never talked of money and assured me that they would make love to me just for fun. I was sure they were decent girls, not prostitutes. Then they tied me up for a laugh... you know... and promised that I would really like what they were going to do to me. At first they were fooling around with me, but then one of them got up and walked around the room. While her friend was looking after me, I realised she was searching through my jacket and my case. I shouted at them and one of them pulled a knife out at me warning me to keep quiet or else... They slapped me and scratched me, then they got up and left in a hurry! Damned bitches!"

Ludwig looked at his reflexion in the mirror, quite abashed and feeling sorry for himself.

"Oh! *Mein Gott,* what will I tell my wife?"

He looked at me then smiled sheepishly:

"Very stupid Ludwig Eh! Very stupid! Akh! These French women!"

"Good night, Ludwig," I deadpanned. "I suggest you have a good shower and get some sleep."

At least Ludwig had been clear-minded and honest enough to blame himself for his disastrous night.

Moral of the story: When in places of which one has little or no experience, it sometimes helps to listen to those who might know better.

———

TWELVE AASTERS?

My wife, Michelle, is French. Worse than that, she's Parisian. She may have taken lessons from General De Gaulle himself in self-righteousness and haughtiness. She dismisses people who don't share her opinions and never admits to being wrong! This unflinching self-confidence sometimes plays tricks on her.

The year had been good. I had been promoted and the company had asked me to participate in a major business conference. This had worried me because, at the time, conferences related to our particular trade were usually in cold and grimy industrial towns and were more a punishment than a reward but, for once, the place was sunny California. As an additional munificent gesture, the management had offered a flight ticket to my wife and had granted us a full month's holiday in the US. This was unheard of in our stingy company, and I was overjoyed. We decided to stop at a few places on the way to the West Coast.

We were newly married, had no children and, although often strong willed and stubborn, Michelle was still the sweet and pretty young thing I had fallen for. In those days, I was eager to satisfy her slightest whims, oddest wishes and most bizarre eccentricities. We loved jazz, so a visit to New Orleans, the legendary capital of rhythm and blues was planned. We could not wait to discover the bayous, the old cotton farms, Creole food and, of course, the jazz clubs.

Like any self-respecting French citizen, Michelle loves to eat and, like most French people, she eats some things uncooked, for instance, raw meat. Another of her favourite meals consists of sea shells and, in particular, raw oysters. When in a restaurant on the ocean front, she will quickly gulp down twelve oysters. Without much of a pause, she will then select twelve more of another brand, just for the sake of comparison. Then, if nothing stops her, she will finish with another twelve, preferably Gilardo's which cost a fortune even without pearls in them!

Oysters are supposed to be a potent aphrodisiac but alas, having gone through three dozen molluscs and quite a few glasses of wine, the arousing elements of oysters are totally suppressed by the volume of absorbed food so, regarding the romantic part of the evening, I have learned with time that my money was always spent in vain!

Oysters are one of the great delicacies of some New Orleans restaurants.

We had barely checked in at our hotel when Michelle declared she was hungry. This, for her, is no joke and there is no time for fooling around. Food has to be provided fast so we went out in search of a good restaurant. The temperature was ideal. Rising from cellars, music filled the streets with its tantalising rhythms, people lazily strolled along but we had to hurry: Michelle was hungry!

She suddenly stopped at an attractive oyster bar, opened the door and, ignoring the polite American tradition of being shown to your seat, walked straight to the best table by the window and sat down. The waitress was surprised but smiled and kindly welcomed the obvious foreigners to the land. She brought us the menu but there was no need to look at it. We knew what we wanted. I looked up.

"Aasters?" she asked.

I speak reasonable English-English, usually understand East and West coast American but, this time, the Deep Southern brawl defeated me and I wasn't quite sure what the waitress had asked. I responded, questioningly:

"I beg your pardon?"

"Aasters?"

It took a while to register

"Oh yes please, we'd love some oysters."

"Uh, uh! How many?"

I looked at Michelle whose English is not as good as mine and who wasn't quite sure what language was being spoken. I asked in French:

"How many oysters will you eat?"

"That's a stupid question! We'll start with twelve each of course."

"Twelve each please."

The woman looked at me dumb-founded:

"Twelve aasters each? Are you shore?"

"Yes," I answered firmly, "twelve each."

"They're biiiig aasters."

"No problem, what I can't eat my wife will."

The waitress shrugged, obviously worried.

"You want them cooked or raaa?"

Once again, I lost the last word and begged:

"Sorry, say that again?"

A little impatiently, she repeated:

"Cooked or raaa?"

It finally registered what the waitress was saying. I was still a little confused, so I asked Michelle, just to make sure:

"Do you want them cooked or raw?"

My wife looked at me as if she suddenly realized she had married a moron. No French citizen except for the mentally deranged would ever eat cooked oysters. They are gulped down in one go with the hapless mollusc cringing under the lethal sting of lemon juice.

"Cooked!" she scorned in amazement. "These people must be mad! Only barbarians can do such a thing. Cooked oysters! Really!"

"Raaa!" I told the waitress who, by now, was a little impatient.

"Twenty four raaa aasters! Look sir, you should start with three each then if you want more, I'll bring more!"

She left with a shrug, casting her eyes up to heaven. I repeated the statement to Michelle who dismissed the whole thing as below her dignity. I suggested that oysters might be bigger in the US than in France but this was taken as absurd.

"Even if they are bigger, oysters are oysters and, if I can eat thirty six Belons, I can certainly eat twelve New Orleans oysters!"

To lighten the mood, I suggested:

"For every oyster you can't eat, you'll make love to me."

"Don't be silly! You are bound to lose and anyway this climate is too hot and humid for exertion!"

I later much regretted she had not taken up the challenge because I would have had a wild time for weeks. Each of the six oysters brought by the waitress was close to the size of an average European beef steak! This clearly startled Michelle who gasped then looked at the shells wide eyed. True to her never-wrong self, she winked at me and smiled prettily with a sigh of content. She then took a deep breath, picked up a shell in her left hand, seized a fork in her right one, labouriously detached the mollusc from its base and thrust the huge oyster in her mouth, ready to gulp it in one go as she usually did.

Alas, the thing wouldn't go. It was just too big for her gullet! So Michelle munched... but it was soon clear that chewing an oyster was not her thing. She turned pale, gasped for air, shut her eyes and, with an enormous effort of will, swallowed the mouthful! She then opened her watery eyes looking vaguely ill, inhaled deeply then looked at me all daggers out:

"OK, so what? These are not oysters; they are excrements of pregnant whales."

Then, after a few moments of silence, she regained her composure.

"I'll try one of them cooked just because we're here. You can do what you want with the rest."

The waitress came to our table:

"Everything OK?"

"No," I said. "Frankly, we are not used to such big oysters. Could we try one cooked please, just for a taste?"

She smiled mockingly.

"I told you they were biiig aasters! I'll bring two of them grilled."

We ate those as we eat meat in Europe, with knife and fork! I liked the taste but Michelle just could not resign herself to her defeat. As long as lasted our holidays in the US, she never touched another shell.

We never went back to an oyster bar; we had learned our limitation. But we loved the jazz, the bayous, the cotton fields, and the charm of the deep South.

WHERE THE SWISS MATCH UP TO THE FRENCH AT THE CHEATING GAME

The South West of France is a beautiful area with a wealth of wonderful historic old towns such as Angoulême, Bergerac, Agen, Auch… The list is endless. These cities are peaceful and full of charm with their crooked-walled medieval houses, their narrow traffic-free streets and their quiet gardens. Every church, statue and wall exudes centuries of history with their related noble spirits and wicked ghosts.

At different times in these peaceful squares, to the great entertainment of the local population, people were beheaded in public for not crying "God save the King," women were accused of witchcraft and burned at the stake because they refused their favors to the local landlord, noblemen happily butchered one another for the love of a damsel, but, thank goodness, in a huge act of brotherhood, built beautiful cathedrals for the redemption of their sins and the saving of their souls.

Things have fortunately changed since these valiant times and one can today travel peacefully on the high roads without having to worry about bandits or starving fanatics armed with picks, axes, and burning torches to steal your sword or your horse or test your unconditional loyalty to the Faith.

One thing has not changed in the South-West of France since the Druid priests: the love and devotion of the local population to superb wines and good food. These are still the essence of life and the major reason for the peaceful and jolly nature of most local residents.

The wish to join this happy brotherhood of good living can lead the unsuspecting foreign traveler to unexpected situations.

One of our customers had his engineering business in Angouleme, in the middle of wine country. I went there often because people were hospitable and friendly, business was growing without effort and also because the place was so out of reach that the trip meant four full days without the hassle and abuse which was the order of things in the office.

Early October is a wonderful period to visit in the area. The light is of that mellow golden quality which makes you feel in paradise; summer heat has been replaced by a heavenly temperature in which one floats in weightlessness, noisy and excited tourists have returned to their toils and one benefits from the local people's relaxed and amiable manners. Vineyards extend for miles, their heavy grapes full of the nectar of the gods. Leaves vary in color from light green and bright yellow to a rich golden brown which, at sunset, gives the impression of fields on fire, their colorful flames swaying gently in the evening breeze.

The atmosphere is not conducive to work and, on that particular trip, once my visit over, rather than suffer the boredom of four hours' train ride to Paris then an hour's flight to Geneva, I rented a car to drive home, a leisurely six hundred miles of country roads through rural France. The rental company had given me a vehicle with Swiss number plates, too happy to find a lunatic ready to drive one thousand kilometers to return the car to its starting point.

October is the season of harvest and pressing of the grapes. Hundreds of people, many dressed in traditional costumes, work in the vineyards. They pick the grapes and, in an elegant gesture, toss them into the wooden basket secured on their back. Along the road, wine-tasting kiosks invite motorists to stop to savor the result of last year's harvest and of older vintage wines.

I am not much of a drinker but, being a French gourmet, my sweet wife loves a good wine, so I decided to surprise her with a case of the very best wine I could find on the way.

I stopped at a kiosk with a colorful tent and was greeted by a pretty medieval wench who handed me a glass of white nectar. After a word of thanks and a smile, I went through the ceremonious motions of a confirmed wine taster: turned the glass in my hand to assess the wine's "tears," inspiringly smelled its fragrance, held up the glass to check its color and transparency then, at long last, took a sip, turning and clicking my tongue in appreciation. The wine was delicious, rich, full and perfect. This was the liquor which would turn my touchy lioness into a tender and purring pussy cat ready to lovingly greet her lord and master in fitting fashion upon his return from far away and perilous travels!

After the tasting, much to my regret, the smiling wench was pushed aside by a fat, rubicund gentleman who asked me in unctuous tones whether I liked the wine.

"Yes, I replied, it is delicious. I will take a case of twelve bottles."

"Ah! Monsieur, just by looking at your expert way of tasting the wine, I knew you were a real connoisseur. You have made the best possible choice. "Clos des Cerfs" is a superb wine and the vintage you have tasted is the best we've had for years."

I was flattered to distraction, asked the price, gulped, haggled, managed to reduce it by thirty per cent, paid, opened the car boot and, proud as a turkey, left with twelve bottles of the best wine in France. I drove less than fifty yards before returning to my senses. Slamming the brakes I reversed at high speed back to the kiosk. Had my rubicund friend given me the same wine as the one I had tasted? His friendliness, confidential tones and above all, his readiness to reduce its price were highly suspect.

I got out of the car and walked up to the man who was going through his routine with another passing motorist.

He looked at me, lifting his eyebrows in happy surprise.

"I am sure you came back for another case, yes?"

"No," I replied. "I would like to taste one of the bottles you have given me."

A look of hurt anger swept his face.

"So, you think I cheated you?" he said loudly. His voice now full and angry, he called the people around him as witnesses. "You think that the honest French wine growers are as crooked as your own Swiss bankers? This is an insult!"

"Now friend! Relax! All I asked was to taste the wine you just sold me. Is there anything wrong in this?"

The man weighed his chances. The onlookers appeared to accept my reasoning. He looked at me suspiciously and beckoned me away from the kiosk.

"You are not Swiss, are you?"

"No, but what's that got to do with it?"

"Your car has Swiss number plates."

"So? How is this related to tasting the wine?"

"Well," he said with a sigh, "if we can't get rid of our plonk on the tourists, who will we sell it to?"

He asked me to move the car to a little wooden shack, away from the road. He went inside, returned with a case of bottles and asked me to open the boot. He took the first case out, dumped it on the ground and replaced it with the new bottles which he very gently set in place.

"You can go in peace. This is the same wine as the one you've tasted. Please, drive carefully so as not to shake it too much. It's precious wine. Oh! And next time you stop, do let us know that you are not a tourist. *Merci et bon voyage.*"

The wine I brought back to Michelle was delicious. She loved it, retracted her claws, melted and, as expected, expressed in pleasing ways her love to her Lord and Master.

Ah! Another successful business trip!

CHAPTER 3

CHARACTERS

Some traveling salesmen have a hobby or a passion to which they cannot resist, even sometimes at the risk of losing their job. Few professionals reach these extremes, but as I studied this behavior, I concluded that they could all be neatly categorized as either one of the Seven Deadly Sins or the corresponding Seven Virtues. They were sometimes embarrassing, often amusing, but for those under their spells, these frenzies were overpowering.

THE FOOD BUFF

Raymond is a good natured and jolly character whose major interest in life is to discover renowned chefs' culinary specialities and taste their best wines.

His physical appearance and, more specifically, the imposing size of his abdomen and posterior betray his passion. He is proud of these telling attributes and considers the mere mention of a slimming diet as an insult to his Creator's will.

Raymond's dream was to be the Quality Supervisor for one of the more reputable "good-food" guides but, failing access to this nirvana, he joined our company as a technical specialist.

Business Travel Can Be Fun

He would plan his trips according to the Michelin guide and was ready to drive hundreds of miles out of his way to satisfy his passion. For the common mortal, travelling with him could sometimes be a wearying experience.

In the thick of winter, one of our customers whose factory was located in France's cold Jura Mountains, reported a problem relating to our product. I did not fancy the trip or the meeting which promised to be difficult, since the client was right and our company had no short-term solution to the defect. Raymond was the only man in our group technically competent enough to discuss the situation and hopefully able to pacify our disgruntled client. My dear fat friend performed at his best after a good meal, so I arranged our visit for the afternoon. True to his passion, Raymond insisted that we have lunch in a two-star restaurant renowned for its sauces "à la Provençale" located over eighty miles from our meeting location.

He started his lunch with "escargots" then, making sure he did not miss one of the Chef's specialities, continued with frog legs served in a rich onion and garlic sauce. Well-fed and happy, Raymond was ready to face the ordeal.

It was freezing cold, windy and pouring with rain, but, driving to the factory the stench in the car was such, due to Raymond's contented belches, that I was compelled to open the windows.

We were coolly received by the boss' secretary who led us to the corner office.

Jolly as ever and oblivious to the unfriendly reception, Raymond warmly returned the client's chilly greeting, enthusiastically shaking his hand while blowing his potent breath in the man's face. The customer reeled under the stench and quickly sat as far as possible from my colleague's lethal exhalations.

No self-respecting Frenchman would condemn anybody for having a good meal but clearly, the consequences of Raymond's lunch were distressing. Utterly put off by the profusion of contented belches, our client completely lost his train of thought and, after a while, unable to take it any longer, got up and opened all the office windows.

Soon after, beside himself with impatience, his teeth chattering with cold, he showed us to the door alleging an urgent meeting and assured us that he would find his own solution to the problem with no need for further assistance.

Raymond was a charming, lovable person who wouldn't harm a flea, but unfortunately, he was a victim of his passion. His business performance could not justify his exceptionally high food bills, and he soon left us to return to his native Belgium.

THE TRAVELLING SAINT

With much the same single mindedness, the pious traveller is totally dedicated to his passion, his religion. When away from home, obeying sacred requirements often imposes planning and determination. Our devout travelling brethren have several advantages over us, miscreants. They are infinitely patient, tolerant, honest, and usually highly respected by their customers.

I met Peter at university. His rich accent with heavily rolling R's was indubitably from the heart of rural Scotland. The eighth son of a Quaker family, he was a brilliant engineering student and shamed us all by his exceptional intelligence and his sobriety. Although he lived on a limited government grant, Peter was always a model of kindness, generosity and good humour. After graduation, we each went our separate ways, and I lost track of him.

Several decades later, after concluding a rewarding contract, I was relishing a succulent meal with a group of managers in one of France's best restaurants. Our noisy table took indecent advantage of our success through an absurdly high entertainment budget while, all around us, other guests noisily celebrated a holy mass to Bacchus and Epicure.

Oblivious to the heathen crowd, a man sat alone at a table, slowly munching through a plate of boiled potatoes while reading a book. His demeanour seemed familiar and the way he was totally immersed in his reading brought back to memory a long forgotten picture. To satisfy my curiosity, I got up and walked up to the gentleman:

"Excuse me sir, are you Peter McTaggart?"

The man briefly looked up, blinked in recognition, attempted a friendly smile but did not stop his silent recitation of the psalm he was reading. Closing his eyes and frowning in concentration, Peter placed his index on his lips begging for silence, postponing a possible conversation until after the end of his prayer. I smiled back and, restraining my joy at running into an old friend, returned to my table baffled and subdued. What was a man of his sobriety and temperance doing in such a bedevilled place, I wondered.

After a while, Peter beckoned me to join him. He hugged me enthusiastically and his warm hearty laughter covered the surrounding noise. He was the export manager of a British company and was a frequent traveller. When away from home, his daily schedule was rigid: up at five thirty, he would say his morning prayers, eat his frugal breakfast then go to his business meetings. He would invariably eat lunch alone before his afternoon appointments after which he would return to his lodgings, located in houses of people of his own religion. He would of course, never go out in the evenings.

Even though that level of devotion was beyond anything I would be capable of, I could admire it greatly. I was truly amazed by Peter's unwavering ways and wondered how a normal man could so steadfastly and single-mindedly resist the many frivolous temptations offered to the traveller in foreign lands.

Full of respect, I begged my old friend to add my name to the long list of people who needed more prayers than I could ever say to save their souls.

THE SEX MANIAC

Then there was Franco. His and Peter McTaggart's passions couldn't be more diametrically opposed.

Most of us have probably travelled with a colleague who is forever chasing women. We may also have wished, at one time or another, to follow his example but faithfulness, self-consciousness, fear of illness, or just a good sense of what's right, have held us back from joining our friend's pursuit of lust.

Franco is good-natured, hedonistic, and very macho, but full of spirit with an infinite fund of jokes to tell. His customers and colleagues enjoy his company, albeit for short periods.

Our firm had a large stand at a major professional fair in Singapore. The attendance was such that our travel agents were unable to find enough single rooms for our delegation, so we had to share our accommodation with a colleague. My room-mate was Franco and I hence had a direct view of his elaborate preparation as a professional seducer.

The young man loved being assigned to our company's shows at trade fairs. Once the stand was erected and our products displayed, his schedule became hectic.

His first hours were devoted to the enthusiastic visit of other displays. This was not for the purpose of spying on our competitors' offers but aimed at finding what he qualified as his own brand of "products."

To avoid the management's loitering ears and hence their wrath at his endless sex-talk, Franco referred to his conquests as "products" and for his everlasting Don Juan stories, used all the engineering vocabulary related to the term.

The stands he visited were carefully selected according to the number, looks and physical attributes of the essential subjects of his interest, their hostesses. Franco walked to the most promising areas with a charming smile and diligently asked introductory questions while his eyes wandered over the various damsels' lips, eyes, chest and legs. His preliminary evaluation completed, he then concentrated on the specific "product" he had assessed as having the shortest "delivery time" and the most promising "performance."

Hence, once "the right product" was found, Franco tried his best to secure an evening's appointment with the lady using his most enticing "Latin lover" charm. This major step successfully completed, he hurriedly collected our competitors' promotional literature, displayed on their stands, to show our delegation manager that he had masterfully carried out his official duties of market-spying activities.

From then on, he was a model of business efficiency. He amiably received prospective customers, ably answered their questions and charmed everyone with his high spirits.

From time to time, he left our stand for an alleged break, but diligent as ever, made his way to his evening damsel's location to ensure that she remained under his spell.

As soon as Franco's self-propelled two-legged "sample" left the fair, he frantically helped us to close the stand and scampered off hurriedly to our hotel. I followed him soon after and found my room-mate fresh out of the bathroom, smelling as if he he'd had a shower with a wide mixture of Chanel perfumes. Franco then inspected himself carefully: no pimples on the brow, no black spots on the nose, no budding bristle on the chin... the face was all right. He then turned to the rest. The stomach and sides were maybe a little flabby but would only be revealed to the subject of his interest too late for clear-minded assessment. Franco's "proprietary component" without whose active participation the evening's purpose was pointless, was subject to close inspection and found to be in good working order. Bar an unexpected accident, Franco declared that his night with his beautiful Delilah should go according to plan and conclude successfully.

He carefully dressed in front of the large wall-mirror then spread perfumed cream on his hair which he combed with care. As a finishing touch, he cleaned his right shoe with his left sock and vice-versa and after an appreciative last look, wished me an enjoyable evening and ran off to his appointment.

Franco had reserved a table in a good restaurant with a romantic ambience. With all the fairs Franco had been to, we thought he'd had more than his fair share of fun and that it was time we hard working slaves taught him a lesson. I gathered some colleagues and suggested we go to the same place. Having spotted his table, we sat in a dark corner from where we could watch his seducer's act.

He treated his intended sweetheart with loving care. A few potent aperitifs were followed by a champagne bottle. The meal was accompanied by lots of smiles, caressing of hands and intertwining of legs. The sweet damsel was clearly following the path set by our conquering Don Juan.

There was a small dance floor and three musicians played soft, languorous music. Before dessert, Franco invited his "product now ready for testing" to dance to the slow rhythm being played. Alas, as he walked to the floor, his mobile phone rang. Franco was being called by the big boss who, informed of our prank, was waiting for him at the door of the restaurant. Much to his annoyance, our friend escorted his prey to their table, promising to return within minutes.

As soon as he was out of sight, two of us went to his seat, explained our trick to the girl, convinced her to join us and hence play the part of the enamoured lover with one of our group. After some convincing, she agreed. As Franco came back, he looked around for the young lady and found her in tender embrace with one of his colleagues. He joined us, flustered by the obviously cheap woman's blatant lack of morals and furious at having wasted his talents when he felt so close to successfully concluding his evening.

Eternal Don Juan though he was, Franco was a good engineer. To lighten his now foul mood, we tried to comfort him in reasonable engineering terms. As any good professional knows, the transfer of a product from laboratory (the fair stand) to field test is fraught with hazards. His "product" was abandoned with no supervision and, as often in these cases, had been stolen. Having taken possession of it, we could find no final destination address or unpacking specifications for it and hence gave it to the person of our group most apt to successfully use it. In fact, we had unburdened Franco of a serious problem, that of finding a suitable test-site: his hotel? Her place? A broom cabinet or car as a last resort?

Franco did not appreciate our joke. He made himself scarce, sulked for the rest of the fair and vowed never to trust us again with his amorous secrets.

Many years after our hard-working times, I still hear from Franco. His travelling days now over, he runs a bar with his wife in his native village where he apparently is a doting grandfather and a faithful family man.

It is pleasing to note that addictions and compulsions don't necessarily destroy that which is good at heart.

CHAPTER 4

EXPLOSIVE MIXTURES

My fellow business travelers will probably agree that the best trips are taken alone. You are master of your time and of your encounters and can suit your leisure to your mood with nobody to question your fancies. But life is not always easy and sometimes, one has to bow to the greater powers that be and travel with one's boss or with an unwelcome colleague.

There are few reasons for chiefs to impose their company onto their juniors. Their most frequent motive is that you've found a large business opportunity and the boss wants to be directly involved. In this scenario, you are stuck and have little chance of inserting some fantasy in the trip. Its objective is well-defined and all involved are intent on producing successful short-term results. No space is left for unexpected fun.

Another frequent justification is that your boss wants to travel with you to monitor your performance. If you are on friendly terms, you can take him on your own turf, deal your own cards, program your joint leisure time and make sure he enjoys the trip. You will come out of the ordeal grinning like a baboon holding a ripe banana. If, on the other hand, you could happily do without his company, you can arrange your trip in such a way that he will never again want to travel with you. In this case, knowing some recipes for "explosive mixtures" may be useful.

My definition of "explosive mixtures" is that your unwelcome travel companion and the place or customer you plan to take him to, are likely, for many reasons, which you are the only one to know, to end up on a violent collision course. The carefully planned ordeal should occur so that it is clearly independent of your will. This will ensure that, first, you are not its cause and second, that the distress for the undesirable individual will be such that he will never bother you again. To organize this particular trip requires imagination, nerves of steel, lots of patience and a good sense of humor.

As the old saying goes, paradise is where you have German administration, French cooking, Italian lovers and English humor. Hell is where you have Italian administration, French humor, a German lover and English cooking! This gives you the gist of what "explosive mixtures" can be. Take a Teutonic manager to Italy and you can make him cry with frustration before the end of your first day together and beg you, crawling on his knees, to take him back to base. Take a French manager to England; he will run back to France and leave you to your "steak and kidney pies" or to your "sausages and mash" after the first pub-meal you treat him to!

Travel with your self-confident but aesthetic-conscious American boss to a country where sheep's eyes are a delicacy one cannot refuse, he will probably never set foot on a plane with you again…or send a quick-tempered Italian manager to carry out a long and protracted negotiation with a very patient Chinese businessman, he will first tear his hair off then, bald and bad tempered as a shorn tiger, he will swim back to Italy if he has to. Finally, travel to South America with a coward with a huge ego (or a personal problem) and you are likely never to be bothered by him again!

It is an interesting study in character, but no matter what the circumstance, in the end, the diversity in human behavior is what makes each of us so fascinating.

ROUGH TRIP FOR HERBERT

This is a long and painful story. I give you my word that every detail is true since, in my wildest dreams, I could never have invented any of these events which all happened within twenty-four hours. That day, my intended "explosive mixture" went far beyond anything I imagined.

A newcomer to our company, Herbert had recently been appointed Marketing Director of our department. He was a sharp-voiced, clean-shaven man in his early forties, with a crew cut and steely blue eyes behind his gold, horn-rimmed glasses. To our company's top management, he clearly embodied "the perfect manager."

We, lowly slaves, were surprised by Herbert's frequent change of employers but our betters had patiently explained that this was due to his vast ambition and fast rise to power which had repeatedly upset all who surrounded him in his previous jobs. He was now seeking recognition without attrition and our management was convinced that our wonderful group, known for its team spirit and good performance, would welcome Herbert and thrive under his amiable and able guidance. In short, Herbert was there to stay whether we liked it or not!

Soon after this heart-lifting introduction, I was asked to plan a visit to Italy with him. Herbert had never been to the country and wanted to visit our twelve customers in three days. My explanations as to the geography of Italy, the spread of our customers and the sometimes unreliable means of transport were of little use. These customers represented twenty percent of our department's sales, Herbert had only three days to devote to them, so the equation was clear and simple. There was little space for further discussion.

Planning this trip was a challenge but, with efficient coordination of air travel and hell-for-leather motorway driving, it could be done. We were to start our Italian tour in Naples and work our way up the Italian peninsula to Turin.

Our flight from Geneva was uneventful and Naples welcomed us with clear skies and clement temperature. Herbert enjoyed his supper on the seafront and congratulated me for his room with a balcony on the sea and wonderful view on Mount Vesuvius. All started well.

In the morning, we took a taxi to our appointment which, due to our tight schedule, was to last from nine to twelve sharp before rushing back to the airport to catch our next flight. Ingegnere Francesco, the managing director of the Company we were visiting, had been informed that our schedule was tight and I had begged him to be on time. A very sharp businessman, Francesco spoke little English and although he was extremely courteous and refined, his sense of time was prone to fantasy and quite different from Herbert's.

We arrived at nine sharp and were kindly offered coffee by Francesco's secretary. I do not know whether my reader ever drank a ristretto coffee in Naples. The concoction is not the standard brew known to ordinary mortals and a gulp of it is equivalent to the same weight of sweet-smelling dynamite: hairs stand up on end, hands tremble, feet walk of their own volition and stomachs gurgle operatic arias without previous training!

Herbert downed two cups in quick succession. Five minutes later he was pacing the lounge as if in intensive training for a military parade. He then disappeared in the corridor and soon after, a frantic and breathless secretary ran into the waiting lounge and begged me to kindly restrain my friend from visiting the offices unaccompanied.

An hour after the appointed time, Ingegnere Francesco appeared, all smiles and worldly gestures.

After a cool handshake, Herbert pointedly looked at his watch.

"Did we make a mistake Mister Francesco, or was our meeting at nine this morning?"

"No, no," said Francesco in good humor, "it was nine, no mistake but you know, traffic in Naples is terrible. Some days I get here before nine, some days after. Today, much traffic but no problem, we do quickly our business and you can go."

Francesco's contract was important and we could not leave without it signed and sealed. Sensing our hurry, our shrewd customer protracted the discussion and insisted on a detailed visit of his factory. Herbert's jaws were clenched and his eyes shot daggers, but it was clear that, unless we played the game by Francesco's rules, we would leave empty handed.

A good deal can only be concluded in Naples over lunch or supper. We had, by then, missed our scheduled flight and, having no alternative, accepted our host's invitation. By mid-afternoon, we were bloated and a little tipsy and time was more for a civilised siesta than for a flight to our next meeting. But business was business and Herbert was Herbert, so we bade goodbye and asked for a taxi to the airport. But, a true Neapolitan and a gracious host, Francesco would not to let us leave without a generous supply of mozzarella cheese, a unique local delicacy.

In most countries, mozzarella found in supermarkets comes as a tasteless white chewy lump the size of a tennis ball, preserved in a thick plastic bag full of water. The real Neapolitan product is quite different in color, texture and taste. It is made in local farms from buffalo milk, has a rich and strong taste and melts in your mouth. The product has one drawback: however well you preserve it, it lasts no more than three days before losing its taste and rotting away. In its home country, the cheese is found in specialty stores, fresh from the day, and is kept in large buckets where it swims in gallons of whey. Upon purchase, the cheese is ladled in a skimpy plastic bag with a generous quantity of liquid. The bag is then simply closed by tying its end in a knot. As a special favor to travelers who ask for it, the first bag is placed in a second one which is just as flimsy as the first.

Our contract successfully signed, a happy Herbert enthusiastically accepted the two large bags of mozzarella offered by Francesco, shook hands and we rushed to the airport to catch the next flight to Milan.

The crowd at the terminal was unusually large, and I sensed something was wrong. An airline hostess fought her way through it, obviously upset. I kindly asked her the reason for the disorder but she shrugged and kept moving without answering. Herbert's direct approach proved more efficient. He grabbed the woman's arm roughly and shouted in her face:

"Hey you! Answer the question! What's happening?"

If looks could kill, Herbert would have died instantly. The hostess jerked her arm free and spat out her words like deadly venom:

"*Che scemo* (what an idiot), strike, airline strike."

This was not new. Strikes of the Italian national carrier were then frequent, and since one could not fight them, the only thing to do was to take them philosophically, with patience and humor. Experience had taught me that a strike in one public sector can spread like wildfire to others, so when in Italy I follow a simple rule: when hit by a strike, I leave the country as fast as I can and by any available means.

I went to an information counter: a Lufthansa flight was due to land half an hour later and return to Frankfurt that same evening immediately after refueling. This was the key to the saving of our bodies if not of our souls. Two seats were available, so I bought the tickets there and then and returned to where Herbert sat in ill-disguised fury.

When I told him that we were going to Frankfurt instead of Milan, he could not believe his ears.

"Frankfurt? What the hell will we do in Frankfurt? And how about all these other meetings?"

I patiently explained the mechanism of strikes in Italy, but he did not believe me.

"You have arranged this trip knowing full well that there would be a strike in the country. Are you trying to show me that working in Italy is difficult? You knew Francesco would be late and that we would miss our scheduled flight! What is this? Are you trying to fool me?"

There was no sense in arguing so I left him alone to seethe in his fury.

The hall was full of people. Children of various ages ran around and played noisily between the exasperated strike-bound passengers. Their tired mothers yelled at them threatening wild beating but to no avail. Fathers shrugged off the problem, oblivious to the whole proceedings. Two aspiring football champions energetically kicked their ball between passengers' legs. Sitting next to their screaming mother, Herbert glared at her as if she were a madwoman out of hell, and very obviously stuck his fingers in his ears to make his feelings clear.

Finally getting tired of the rumpus, a father caught one of the children as he ran. Stopped dead in his game, the child shrieked, writhed, kicked and resisted his father's grip with all his energy. He thrashed about so fiercely that he finally escaped and ran straight into one of Herbert's bags of mozzarella, ripping it open with a loud "bang." A big jet of whey drenched Herbert's trousers, four mozzarella balls gently rolled on the floor, and a slippery puddle formed at my boss' feet.

Totally incensed, Herbert got up and impulsively slapped the bewildered child with a loud clap. The brat screamed; his mother got up, grabbed hold of the first bag within her reach, lifted it and crashed it with a loud bang on Herbert's head, calling him all the names in her vast repertory of insults. While all this happened, I was some distance away, talking to another stranded passenger. I turned around just as the child's father struck an almighty punch on my colleague's unsuspecting chin. Women and children shrieked, men threatened, the crowd closed around Herbert who stood bewildered and uncomprehending in the middle of the pandemonium. The Italians' reaction was obviously past his understanding and he was at a loss as to what to do next.

Herbert was tall and strongly built but, luckily, he was not a fighter. Had he responded to the blow he would have been a dead man. I ran to the battleground and forced my way through the crowd. There was clearly no time for philosophical discussions. I apologized profusely to the offended family, offering the excuse that the way children were brought up in Germany was very different from how it was in Italy and swearing by all the Saints in Heaven that Herbert meant no harm to the child. Confronted by a hostile crowd, it was time for a humble retreat. Red as a beetroot, Herbert collected his case and his remaining mozzarella bag and we hastily walked away to a quieter haven.

We took refuge in the airport restaurant. From our table, we could see the runway and I silently prayed for the speedy arrival of the Lufthansa aircraft. At last, a black dot appeared in the distance and a few moments later, the central carriage wheels of the Boeing 737 puffed their smoke onto the tarmac. We watched the front nose of the plane drop gracefully, and as the front wheel touched down, there was a loud explosion. Thousands of sparks shot up from under the carriage as the aircraft ground to a halt. It looked as if the front tires had exploded. Sometime later, a message on the intercom confirmed that there would be no flight to Frankfurt that night! Our only alternative was a fast drive to Rome International airport with the hope of seats on a flight out to anywhere.

Herbert was past caring! I dragged him down to the rental counter and got a fast car.

Germany is still blessed with no speed limit on its motorways so driving in Italy at two hundred kilometers per hour did not overly worry Herbert. Once in Rome airport, I ran to the foreign airline counters. Alas, the few outgoing flights were fully booked. Even the traditional sorry story of a sick wife awaiting my return had no effect on the harassed personnel.

We passed an Alitalia counter which was deserted except for an employee who was calmly reading his newspaper, comfortably seated in his armchair, feet up on his desk. This was just too much for Herbert. Totally enraged by the man's obvious disregard for his duty, he stopped in front of the counter and crashed his fist on it in fury. The sudden noise made the man jump out of his chair like an epileptic cat. Facing him and airing all his pent up fury, Herbert screamed at him:

"You, ignorant bastard! You lazy dog! You good for nothing blithering idiot! How can you sit there and read your paper when you and your colleagues put thousands of people in trouble? Where are your aeroplanes, where are your flights? You get paid for this job, but you don't deserve your money!"

Initially startled by the unexpected aggression, the man quickly realized that he was facing a dimwit who knew nothing of Italian ways and whose ideas were sadly polluted by notions of hard work and efficiency.

He looked at his assailant with eyes full of pity, moved his face very close to Herbert's, hung his tongue between his lips, filled his cheeks with air and emitted a loud raspberry right in my boss's face, after which he calmly returned to his armchair, sat down, and went back to his reading.

I thought Herbert would have a stroke. Stunned by the Italian's cheek, he fumed like a mad bull, speechless!

I slumped down, defeated, in a nearby armchair. Sometime later, an intercom announced a flight for Milan. I sprang up and prepared to run to the gate but Herbert stopped me:

"Hey, why are you in such a hurry? Forget flying tonight. We will spend the night in Rome and leave tomorrow."

This was not my intention. The latest news was that the strike would continue and that all Italian airports would be closed until further notice. Milan was only four hours' drive from Geneva and, if at all possible, I was leaving Rome that night to get as close as possible to home.

Herbert tried the "Big Boss" act:

"Listen Bob, if I tell you we'll stay in Rome that means that we will both stay in Rome, right?"

"Oh no friend! Out of business hours, you do as you like and I do as I like. Have a good stay in Italy."

I turned and ran to the boarding gate closely followed by Herbert who had thought better of it and was puffing behind me like a crazed bull. We were lucky. By that time, almost everybody had abandoned all hope of flying and there were seats available. Herbert put his case and remaining bag of mozzarella in the luggage rack and slumped in his seat with a sigh of relief.

Shortly after takeoff, a passenger behind us called the stewardess.

"Hey miss! It's raining in the plane."

Because of the change in pressure, Herbert's last mozzarella bag was dripping its smelly water from the luggage rack! The passenger protested, upset by the stench on his suit. Herbert invoked airline insurance, but I thought we'd had enough problems already and to avoid lengthy discussions, I paid for the cleaning of our victim's suit. Other passengers moved to other seats in a hurry!

We landed in Milan well past midnight and took a taxi to my usual hotel. Alas, the place was fully booked as were all good hotels in town. The concierge offered us a comfortable armchair in a private lounge, but Herbert refused this further indignity.

The porter then suggested a small but clean boarding house nearby where they might still have a room.

Once again we picked up our cases and walked our tired bodies down the road to the little hotel. The door was closed. We rang. A large man who looked more like a professional wrestler than an inn-keeper answered our call. He luckily still had two spare rooms but they were to be paid cash in advance.

We were not in a position to argue so we stepped in and dropped our bags at different corners of the small entrance hall. While Herbert rummaged through his attaché case for his passport, I counted our night's money in my wallet.

All of a sudden, I heard a wild shriek and saw a writhing ball of black hair fly unexpectedly right under my nose. The thing crashed, screaming on the floor and what I now saw was a black poodle scampered away whimpering in misery.

Before I could understand what had happened, Herbert's suitcase flew through the air crashing loudly against the hotel door. Shouting obscene swear words at my friend, the big man grabbed Herbert roughly by the nape of the neck and carried him all the way to the door, at the same time vigorously kicking his backside. He opened the door and chucked Herbert out as he would have done with a rag doll, hurling his case at him for good measure.

I thought my final hour had arrived, but could still not understand what had happened. The large man came towards me menacingly:

"If I ever see that bastard again, I'll kill him. Just get the hell out and keep him away from here!"

There was clearly no room for argument so I quickly took my suitcase and left. Outside, Herbert was in shock.

"Now tell me, what happened?" I asked.

It seemed that the porter's little black poodle, which we had not seen in the dark hall had been attracted by Herbert's interesting trousers and had come to sniff them. The scent of mozzarella ingrained in the cloth had so touched his fancy that losing all control, he had gingerly pissed on Herbert's leg. My boss who, at that moment had been filling in his registration form, sensed that something was happening at the bottom of his leg. He looked down, witnessed the animal blissfully squirting on his trousers, and hating dogs anyway, lifted the unsuspecting pet by the belly with his toe, kicked it hard and hurled the helpless poodle two meters up into the air! The porter had summarily avenged his little pet, leading to our sorry state of affairs at well past two o'clock in the morning in a dark street of Milan.

There was little left for us to do but spend the rest of our night in a chair at Linate airport.

Would I call that day "fun?" Certainly not while it lasted but in our company and elsewhere, friends were in stitches as I recounted the unfortunate tales of our friend Herbert.

Herbert never traveled with me again and, as far as I know, never returned to Italy. Less than two years later, he left our company.

It certainly was a lesson in self-righteousness I shall never forget. Travel often requires us to be flexible but some people are too wrapped up in their own importance to ever learn the valuable trait of sharing other folk's emotions.

ENOUGH IS ENOUGH!

Our prospective partner in the Far East was a world class Hong Kong company headed by its founder, Mr. Wong. Although a tough negotiator, Mr. Wong was a friendly individual who was eager to work with us. After long and patient negotiations, initial papers had been drafted for a promising joint venture where he bought our know-how, paid us royalties, and manufactured and sold our equipment in China.

Our chief financial officer and our local office manager were delegated to finalize the few remaining details and sign the final contract. Due to the time gap between

Europe and Hong-Kong, the conclusive meeting was to start at two o'clock in the afternoon to allow, in case of need, a conference call with our Geneva office.

There was no call from Hong Kong that morning so we believed that all had been successfully concluded.

The phone sprang to life late in the afternoon when night was already well advanced in the Far East. Our Italian chief financial officer, a man of excellent professional ability but of fairly short temper, stammered his uncontrolled fury and total bewilderment over ten thousand miles of telephone cable.

The negotiations had irretrievably failed, our prospective partnership was lost and our colleagues had not been able to understand the reason for the unexplained and sudden change in Mr. Wong's attitude.

Marco and Piero had been driven from their hotel to Mr. Wong's corporate headquarters in a luxurious chauffeur driven Rolls-Royce. They had then been dutifully escorted to the conference room which had hosted our earlier negotiations. Tea had been served and the friendly meeting started with Mr. Wong and his assistant, Mr. Wu.

Most outstanding issues had been resolved leaving one last detail relating to the share each company would pay of some minor operational costs.

After much discussion, Marco offered what he felt was a fair deal for each partner. Mr. Wong asked for a further review of the figures. Our colleagues had then exchanged views in Italian to see how low they could go without losing face. During this conversation, Mr. Wong had got up abruptly looking furious, had shouted in Chinese what sounded like very angry words and had stormed out of the room followed by Mr. Wu.

A few minutes later, a secretary curtly asked our two colleagues to leave. Piero and Marco were unsmilingly escorted out of the building, totally bewildered and wondering what had caused Mr. Wong's fury. There was no Rolls-Royce waiting for them and they were left to walk back to their hotel dumbfounded.

During our phone conversation, Marco went through the meeting in detail but to no avail; none of us could understand the reason for its abrupt end. The mystery could only be solved by talking to Mr. Wong himself.

We phoned him but were informed by his secretary that he did not wish to speak to us after the insults and abuse which had been flung at him by our colleagues. We knew that Marco was short-tempered, but he was not rude, so our perplexity was deepened even further. We asked to speak to Mr. Wu, a mild and quiet man who, after a long wait, took our call.

Clearly, even Mr. Wu was upset. He reported that Mr. Wong had been badly insulted and did not wish to continue relations with our company. We asked what the insult had been but Mr. Wu was reluctant to repeat the offending words. Finally, after much polite circumlocutions, he whispered confidentially:

"Mr. Marco twice referred to Mr. Wong as 'bastard' in Italian, thinking that Mr. Wong did not understand."

"Bastard?" Not possible! Never in his most explosive moments had Marco ever referred to anybody as "bastard" during a business meeting. This was even less conceivable during friendly negotiations which were to conclude a mutually advantageous contract.

Totally confused, we called Marco and Piero.

"Marco, have you ever accused Mr. Wong of being a bastard?"

Our two managers were even more bewildered than we were:

"A bastard? Why would we treat Mr. Wong of bastard? The man must be mad!"

There was a long deadly hush on the line, then Piero slowly said:

"I think I understand... but no, it's not possible, it can't be true!"

We listened intently as he went on:

"When Marco spoke to me in Italian, he said that we had gone far enough in our offer. He literally said: *"Adesso basta! Basta! Ci fermiamo qui!"* (Now, enough is enough! That is as far as we'll go!)

Mr. Wong no doubt understood: "He is a bastard, a bastard!" In fact, I remember that it is immediately after our exchange that he got up and left!

How could such a silly word cause such a major business disaster! We tried everything we could think of to re-establish our relations with Mr. Wong: sent him a luxurious dictionary, an expensive watch from Geneva embossed with his name, sought assistance from the local Embassy but to no avail.

Enough was enough ...and *basta*!

Knowing a little of the Chinese mentality, I concluded that Mr. Wong had found a good excuse to get out of a business deal which, after thought, he did not really want. Was our business sector -new to his company- not rewarding enough? Had he received a better offer from a competitor? We will never know.

LOOKING FOR TROUBLE

"The Boss" walked into my office and said genially:

"Bob, you speak Spanish, and I'm sure you also do well in Portuguese. I think you deserve a promotion and have decided to add Latin America to your responsibilities. Come on, great guy, open this continent for us and go show them who we are!"

After which, he winked at me as if he had announced a trebling of my salary and walked out without waiting for an answer.

Though in the company's corridors, I bitched about the insane amount of work this would add to what I already had, I secretly loved the idea of discovering Latin America. I thought that a change of geography and new people to visit would do me good. Before starting off, I gathered information from knowledgeable travelers on each of the places I was planning to visit. Alas, all opinions seemed to concur and I was more than abundantly warned of the dangers of traveling on that continent: kidnappers in Bogota, murderers in Lima, thieves in Rio, rapists in Caracas! There was not a single place I could name without getting a full list of enough heinous crimes to put the whole country's population behind bars! Anyway, before my first trip, the boss duly warned me:

"If I ever hear that, after your meetings, you walk around and visit places in your usual stupid ways on that continent of criminals, I'll sack you without notice! I have enough problems on my desk without having to hire an army of private detectives to look for your dismembered corpse in a ditch and anyway, I wouldn't miss you much if that happened!"

So, duly warned, I took off. After business, I, of course, walked around everywhere, making new friends and discovering new places. I never had a problem anywhere and loved every town I visited.

One of my ambitions was to visit a *favela* (a Brazilian slum) in Rio de Janeiro. These had been described to me as hell on earth infested by brigands and murderers from where no visitor ever came out alive. Much to my disappointment, achieving this ambition was too easy to be what I call "fun."

I took a taxi from the hotel and asked the driver to drop me by the roadside about a kilometer away from the selected favela, which was supposed to be the most dangerous in the area. I walked up to "the gates of hell" in my old jeans and sneakers with nothing on my wrist nor around my neck and with just enough petty cash to buy a drink. I stopped at the first café with chairs on the pavement and asked for tequila. Two men were playing chess on the table next to mine and I intently followed their game. At the end, one of them asked me if I wanted to play. In pidgin Spanish mixed with French and apologizing for my non-existent Portuguese, I happily accepted the challenge of a game which I quickly lost.

This defeat allowed the beginning of a friendly conversation. I explained that I was a French teacher and wanted to check for myself whether the reports one read in Europe about *favelas* was the truth or, as I suspected, a load of rubbish. (In Latin American countries, France still benefits from the aura of the French Revolution with its emblem of "freedom, equality and fraternity." This is how I justify my lie.).

A few minutes later, I embarked upon a grand tour of the land with stops for coffee at every corner where people showed me around, gave me the secrets of their cooking recipes, unveiled details of family problems and neighborly quarrels and commented on the ineptitude of government and politicians. I left the place with a collection of new friends, and the promise that I would return on my next visit to Rio.

After many months of trekking through Latin America, business materialised, customers became friends, the boss started to argue about the costs of travel and the trips became a routine.

The standard tour consisted in leaving Geneva for Buenos Aires on a Saturday morning to benefit from the luxury of a Sunday afternoon's rest before starting the working week. The trip continued to Santiago de Chile, Lima in Peru, Bogotá in Columbia, Caracas in Venezuela and ended with San Paolo in Brazil before flying back to Geneva, crawling on all fours, as fresh as a rotten fish! Sometimes, Bolivia, Puerto-Rico and Mexico were also thrown in just to remind me that, if my current customers did not bring us enough orders to satisfy the South American forecast, there were still many markets which needed our company's urgent attention.

After a time, I had enough flying bonus points to fly me free of charge either to Mars and back or to the nearest cemetery, but, alas I was neither allowed time off for a well-deserved holiday, nor for an eternal peaceful rest! So I went on strike and would not budge from the office until the boss had hired a full-time manager to look after the Latin American markets.

In my innocence, I had forgotten that hiring a man meant an insane amount of paperwork: recalculation of sales forecasts, re-crunching of the figures expected for costs and revenue and all the related pure fiction which is the order of things to justify the increased expenses of a new salesman. No matter how large the profit forecasts were invented to be, the boss's wailing would be heard all the way to Timbuktu!

I finally won the day and we hired Jo, an American of Cuban origin, who lived in Miami. Jo knew our business well. He had been responsible for the South American market with one of our competitors and appeared to be a sure bet for increasing our revenue in the area. He was a stocky, jocular and happy character who admitted to doing about as much sport as a pregnant hippo and who made it quite clear to us that he liked his food, drinks, and siesta after lunch.

After a period of training at headquarters, we planned a trip together to visit our Latin American customers. During our many conversations before the trip, I had been surprised to discover that, although Jo had travelled to all the places I had visited, he did not seem to know the sights, the fascinating museums which can always be visited between two business calls, or the beautiful monuments which, at worst, can be seen from a taxi window. This puzzled me but, since I did not want to hurt my new colleague, I avoided comments on what I considered a surprising lack of curiosity.

He coming from Miami and me from Geneva, our meeting place was a modern and, as far as I knew, peaceful capital with a pleasant traffic-free area where one could lazily stroll during the evening. After our day's work we returned to the hotel, an ancient "Palacio" on the town's major square opposite the country's presidential palace. I asked Jo:

"Shall we have a shower and meet in an hour in the lobby? We'll then go for a walk and find a restaurant on the way."

"A walk?" said Jo in alarm, "Where do you want to walk to?"

"Nowhere in particular, just around town until we find a restaurant we like."

"What's wrong with taking a taxi to the best place in the city?"

"Nothing," I answered, "but it's a pleasant evening and I'd like to stretch my legs."

"The place is dangerous, I never walk anywhere."

"So what do you do in the evenings when you don't have a business appointment?"

"I have my food and drinks brought to my room and eat in front of TV."

"Uh! Not my style. How about trying something new for a change?"

"OK," he said, "but I warn you! We are sure to have trouble."

"Well, I've never had any trouble so far. To avoid problems, I suggest you start by removing your expensive watch from your wrist."

"But how will I know the time?" he answered in alarm.

"Why would you need to know the time? We're not busy or in a hurry. We'll eat when we please then come back when we're tired. At worst, if you're really anxious, we'll ask."

Jo didn't seem convinced and shrugged:

"Nah! I'll keep my watch. It's a cheap one!"

"Yes, of course, we both know that, but for anybody who doesn't know, it looks expensive."

But Jo was stubborn and kept his watch.

"And something else," I added. "Instead of leaving your wallet in your back pocket where it's a real invitation to theft, put some small bills and a credit card in your side pocket and leave the rest behind."

"What if we are attacked? My wallet contains all my papers and the police will know who I am if we are aggressed."

I did not want to hurt Jo so I said nothing, knowing in advance that with such a blatant exhibition of his riches, we were indeed inviting trouble.

We strolled peacefully to an attractive restaurant and my new friend was starting to warm-up to the idea that, maybe, the city was indeed a civilized place.

Supper was excellent and after more than a few glasses of wine, Jo was extremely happy. We walked back to the hotel. The temperature was ideal, people were chatting on benches or strolling idly looking at the attractive shop windows. Children were playing football in the side lanes and time flowed peacefully.

One of the children playing football ran towards us and jumping merrily, asked:

"Mister, Mister give me a dollar, give me a dollar..."

He then stopped and genially pointed at Jo's wrist:

"What time, what time?"

Taken by surprise, but in a relaxed mood, Jo looked at his watch ready to answer, when suddenly he felt a hand grab his wallet in his back pocket. Realising he'd been tricked, he turned around and yelled:

"Son of a bitch!"

The children had now surrounded us. Fast as lightning and lithe as a monkey, a third child jumped on Jo's back to further distract his attention. It all happened so fast in this quiet environment that, unsuspecting as I was, I was taken by surprise. By the time I'd realized what was happening, the children were running away in all directions, racing between the many strollers and vanishing like ghosts. I ran like a madman after one of them and, as luck would have it, he was the one holding the wallet. Feeling me hot on his trail, he dropped it and raced off as fast as his little legs could carry him.

I picked it up and, relieved, brought it back to Jo who was puffing and steaming, his eyes bulging out of their orbits, his nostrils fuming vitriol.

"I told you!" he screamed. "You can't trust these sons of bitches. They're criminals, just damned criminals. I should never have listened to you and stayed in the hotel."

"OK," I conceded, "let's check for what's missing. You've got your watch? Good! Anything missing in the wallet?"

Jo carefully checked everything.

"The little bastard didn't have time to go through it. He only took a few dollar bills."

"Well, we're lucky. No loss of credit card, no great loss of money, no broken bones. In fact, all is okay, so just take it as a little bit of excitement. Next time we'll know better: no watch, no wallet and everything will be fine."

"There will be no f…..g next time for me! If you want to get killed, that's your problem. I'll stay in the hotel. At least I won't have to worry about these damned criminals."

After another few hundred yards of uneventful walking and my pacifying words, Jo seemed to relax. We reached the large square where the Presidential Palace stood opposite our hotel. Located slightly off the crowded shopping area, the square was practically empty except for a shrivelled little man with a hat in one hand and a bottle in the other, sitting on a bench, totally dedicated to the pleasure of drinking his wine in long gulps. We avoided the bench but, slowly focusing on us, the man got up and walked unsteadily towards us. I hurried away, wishing to avoid him at all cost. The man was small, of slight build and obviously very drunk. Jo muttered:

"Well, if he wants a fight, he'll get a fight, filthy ignorant drunkard!"

"Forget it Jo. If he speaks to us, just ignore him and keep walking."

But Jo needed to avenge himself on somebody for his earlier mishap and looked challengingly at the drunkard. Sure enough, while still a short distance from us, the man shouted in uncertain tones:

"Hey you! Salute our President when you walk by his Palace."

I sped along. Jo faced the man and shouted back:

"Your President can kiss my arse, you drunken bastard."

The man stopped, downed his remaining wine then, fast as lightning, deftly threw his bottle with all his strength, aiming straight at Jo's head. He barely missed and the bottle crashed a few yards away. Jo ran to the tattered glass, picked up some pieces and aimed at the drunkard. I raced towards him, grabbed his arm, shook him with all my strength and screamed:

"Stop you raving idiot, you'll have us either jailed or killed."

Attracted by the noise, people gathered around us wondering what the commotion was about, while the drunken sharp shooter was shouting at the top of his voice, pointing at Jo:

"That gringo insulted our President, that gringo insulted our President!"

Time for a gentle stroll was over, I screamed at Jo:

"Get moving, I'll see you in the lobby."

Jo was still not sure whether to teach the drunkard a lesson or to save his own skin. He finally thought better of it and puffing and wheezing like an old steam roller, he ran back to the hotel.

By that time, there was nearly a revolution in the square and I was afraid people would call the police to protest about the insulting behavior of the fat gringo.

Thankfully, the man was so drunk that, in the end, people just ignored him.

We survived, but I never walked again with Jo in Latin America's peaceful and friendly downtowns.

I learned later that Jo was, unfortunately, an alcoholic, and that helped me understand why he lashed out so horribly at the harmless drunk on the Plaza. But, as said earlier, there are people with whom one should not travel.

MEETING THE ASSASSINS

Sometimes what is expected to be an explosive mixture turns out to be an unexpectedly enriching adventure.

Business took me to Alexandria, in Egypt. My family lived there for some years, and I have very fond memories of my childhood in this great city.

Egyptians are wonderful people. They are humorous, cheerful, hospitable, polite, but regrettably for them, are burdened by an incredibly heavy, slow and disorganized administration. To do business in Egypt, you need the patience of the Prophet Job. The intricate and endless procedures added to the incredibly slow decisional processes are maddening.

In the course of my earlier trips, I had visited all the interesting highlights of Alexandria and its surroundings and now, patiently waiting for an eventual decision, I faced two days of doing nothing.

When we lived in the city, some neighborhoods were considered dangerous. They were the very poor "Arab quarters" where, according to my parents, lurked sinister and famished people, ready to slay anybody who showed the slightest trace of wealth.

We often went to the idyllic beach of Agami but to get there, we had to cross these poor districts. We children were then compelled to close all the car windows and the chauffeur sped, honking, through the perilous streets of these ill reputed areas.

Bored and aimless, I decided to tempt fate and discover these haunts of brigands. If I had to die, I preferred assassination to boredom. It would be faster and would release me from the responsibility of suicide. To speed up my inevitable demise, I even decided to take pictures. Adult Egyptians hating being photographed, I was certain to meet with a quick end.

The Street of the Seven Sisters is the gateway to the hellish districts. It is a relatively narrow street lined by ancient houses which shudder at every passage of an old clanging tramway.

At the street's entrance, an old carter was unhurriedly unloading wood planks off his cart in the midst of mind-boggling traffic while his donkey rummaged with delight in a large refuse bin within its reach. I just had to photograph this bucolic scene in the midst of the ambient chaos.

Apprehensive, carefully hiding behind a parked van across the street to get my tablet out of its case, I took many pictures of the donkey and the cart driver. So far, no one had assailed me.

Proud of my feat, I walked a little further through the abundance of tradesmen stalls and wide assortment of artisans' workshops. A street vendor of various drinks pushed his colorful wooden cart in the narrow passage between the tram rails. Fixed on the cart were five large gleaming vessels each containing a delicious nectar: orange or mango juice, hibiscus-flower tea (*karkadeh*, an Egyptian specialty), orgeat syrup and iced tea. The man announced his arrival by clanging two metal cymbals one against the other. This ear-piercing rattle dominated the ambient hum. Customers quenched their thirst in the middle of the street, indifferent to the impatient honking of motorists wishing to pass. Hiding behind a telegraph pole, I, once again, shot the picturesque scene. So far, I was still alive!

Driven by curiosity, I entered a narrow lane perpendicular to the Seven Sisters Street. I was here at the heart of the assassins' quarter which so frightened my parents.

In these narrow alleys, there was no place to hide. The clay-surfaced passage was dingy, lined with antique houses dating back to the 19th century when Egypt was still under the jurisdiction of the Ottoman Empire.

One of the houses still had a *moucharrabieh*, the overhanging balconies with wooden trellis from which, locked-up by their jealous husbands, women could look down in the street without being seen.

It was unthinkable for me not to photograph such wonders.

Sitting on an old chair, a man was serenely smoking his hookah in front of his junk-shop. I asked him:

"May I take photos in this street, please?"

"There's nothing to see here. Go take pictures elsewhere!" was the gruff answer.

I let a moment pass then, sighing, added, "It's a pity! The old houses are beautiful. In a few years, they will all be replaced by tall twenty five floors buildings like the one that already sprung over there, at the very end of the street. There will only be you and me to remember ancient times this beautiful alley.

The man stopped smoking and thought for a moment.

"You are unfortunately right. But tell me, what will you do with those photos?"

"I'll put them in an album so that our children can see the beautiful Alexandria of ancient times that you and I have known."

"By Allah! What a good idea! Go ahead, take all the pictures you want except me. I don't wish my face to be in your book. When you've finished here, I'll take you to other old streets in the neighborhood."

And so, thanks to my new friend, I walked around the ancient quarters of Labban and Gabbari, the dangerous bandits' haunts. In a nearby alley, one of the buildings had partially collapsed. This did not stop families from living in the part still miraculously standing. The people had put their clothes to dry on ropes strung between posts planted in the rubble of the collapsed part. This allowed them to reach their dried washing from their rickety balcony without leaving their apartment. I said to my guide:

"Living in this building is very dangerous. The standing part is sure to collapse soon."

"Amr Allah! It will be the will of God." he answered in typical Egyptian fatalistic character.

I met many people. They all exuded kindness, courtesy and love of life. I was invited to have coffee and shisha (hooka) at every street corner and encouraged to take pictures everywhere, even where there was nothing worth remembering.

After a while, I finally met murderers, real ones whose reputation so terrified my elders! They were hospitable, courteous, cheerful and proudly walked me to the areas of their great massacres.

These were makeshift pens in a small square where sheep and cows peacefully grazed their ample supply of alfalfa.

The day was the eve of Eid al Adha, the Muslim feast which celebrates the sacrifice of Abraham. Founder of the three monotheistic religions, "Ibrahim" is highly venerated in Islam. The event glorifies God's restraining of the Prophet's arm, when this was ready to slay his son Isaac in obedience to the Lord's command. Seeing that Abraham was ready to slaughter his own son to prove his Faith, Isaac was instantly replaced by the sacrificial lamb.

On the occasion of the Eid, countless sheep and cattle are slaughtered. When we lived in Alexandria, a majority of them were killed in slaughterhouses. Today, in a much more Islamic Egypt than in our time, nearly all the slitting of throats is carried out in the streets, under the eyes of passers by and, more dramatically, in full view of the animals awaiting their fate, bleating and mooing heartbreakingly in their pens.

The "murderers" were just street butchers doing their grim job whose reputations, in earlier days, had been highly distorted and wildly magnified.

During my visit, they kindly invited me to share their meal and to come, without fail, to the banquet they would offer to all visitors on the following day.

I did not stay in Alexandria for the Eid. I had reached my goal: see and talk to the people who so anguished many Europeans who then lived in the city. Despite their gruesome but respectable job, the "assassins" were perfectly amiable human beings. One just had to conquer their trust to uncover the kindness of their heart.

CHAPTER 5

NAPLES, PARADISE OF BUSINESS ADVENTURERS

Naples, the largest city in southern Italy, is better known as a starting point for sunny and lazy holidays in Capri and Sorrento than as a prime destination for businessmen. Yet the region is one of the most sophisticated industrial centers in the country. Anybody looking for a weekly shipment of a thousand tons of spaghetti, the transfer of technology for a ground coffee factory, sophisticated satellite electronics or futuristic telecommunication equipment is likely to find it in one of the little known modern companies operating in the area.

The city was founded by ancient Greeks some 500 years B.C. They were later overpowered by the Roman imperialists who found the place so attractive that their richer citizens rushed to it for their holidays. Amongst others, Emperors Tiberius, Caligula, Claudius, and Nero had their summer villas on one or the other of Naples bay's many beaches where they gave wild parties for their mistresses and minions, murdered their obnoxious mothers and slowly roasted their slovenly slaves whose horrible screams were accompanied by the heavenly sounds of the harps.

Mount Vesuvius, the temperamental native volcano, evened out all ethnic feuds and family squabbles by blowing up in the year 79, showering the area with burning cinders. All those who built their homes on its slopes without proper building permits (a national sport in Naples, much like their avowed disregard for traffic laws) as well as decent law abiding citizens, whether Greek or Roman, masters or slaves, virgins or prostitutes, were petrified for eternity during their lazy afternoon friendly card game, manly drinking party or languorous love-making.

But Neapolitans never learn and not even the vicious explosion of their angry mountain discouraged them from rebuilding their houses on its sunny, lazy wine growing slopes where love is said to be more passionate than anywhere else in the world.

After the fall of the Roman Empire, Naples was invaded by every living conquistador under the sun: Byzantine emperors, Vandals and Saracens were followed by bearded Normans who confirmed that, unlike their own unemotional blonds, Neapolitan wenches took their temperament after the local volcano and were too good to be left to others. But, like their predecessors in the land, the mighty Vikings soon grew lazy and, since then as today, word of happy sex spreads quickly among men, many people rushed forth to sample the local talent. Most eager of all were the lusty French Angiovine kings who descended upon Naples where they settled for two centuries, starting in 1266.

The French are not known for sharing their food and good living freely. True to their reputation, they shielded their Neapolitan wine and women from the thieving eyes of the heathen by keeping them behind six foot thick walls of their castles which, still impressively surround the city today.

But all good things come to an end and the Spanish House of Aragon spoiled all the fun with their religious fanaticism and their search for eternal saintliness. They conquered the heathen town and held the city on a tight leash for over four centuries, until the time that Napoleon's handsome and extravagant brother-in-law, General Murat, decided to give back to Naples some of its carefree sparkle.

Throughout their tormented history, the Neapolitans commiserated, lamented, shouted and revolted and in the end, tired of being ordered about by accursed foreigners, lived their own lives and did their own thing regardless of who were the temporary masters of their destinies. They had learned from long experience that proud conquerors, whatever their origin, would, in the end, always succumb to the region's own brand of lethal virus: *Dolce farniente!*

Over the centuries, Neapolitans produced, amongst other, a vast number of brilliant writers, musicians and painters. They learned to sing, dance, drink and enjoy life under the worst predicaments. The result of this rich and painful history is that Naples is Naples and Neapolitans are Neapolitans, a unique blend of genius, fantasy, humor and treachery born from the need to survive with a smile and thrive under all circumstances.

In our modern industrial society, Neapolitans are the closest archetypes of what I would call "free men." Many of them, whether rich or poor, manage to do what they want, when they want, how they want, a luxury long forgotten in our organized world. This is the reason I consider Naples a paradise of adventure for anybody who is ready to accept disorganization and anarchy as a way of life, to laugh at himself when taken for a long ride, and to enjoy the present moment even in the most unexpected situations.

FIRST TIME IN NAPLES

July called for my quarterly trip to Naples for a visit to my good friend Ingegniere Francesco, the director who so successfully managed to frustrate my manager Herbert on that most fateful trip I relayed earlier.

During summer, the planes were full of holiday-makers coming from or going to the beaches. Noisy families had their hands full of bags with children's plastic boats, pails and rakes and ample supplies of wine, salami, cheese and bread loaves. These goodies had either been given by parents or friends on departure or were brought as gifts to parents or friends on arrival.

Traveling in this pandemonium with a suit and an attaché case, I felt like a lone penguin in a herd of frolicking cows. In this noisy human tide, through ignorance or misfortune, if you were not among the first on board, the only way to secure a reasonable seat was to take a deep breath, pull in your stomach, carry your attaché case on top of your head and, with apologies for your manners written all over your face, to forcefully edge your way between carton bags, nets of foodstuff, large bottoms, and screaming kids.

I finally made it to my seat and slumped uncomfortably into it with my knees doubled up to my chin. As usual, I buried myself in a book, impervious to the surrounding pandemonium. The quiet, elderly couple sitting next to me spoke English.

"I'll be glad when we get there", he said affectionately patting his wife's hand. "It's been a long trip."

"Our life's dream has finally come true", she answered with a contented sigh.

She looked at me and smiled prettily. I smiled back:

"Going to Naples for the first time?" I asked.

"Yes! Both our families originate from Naples. We are third generation Americans, we live in Cincinnati and our dream has always been to return to our families cradle."

"Do you still have relatives in Naples?"

"Yes but we've never met nor even spoken to them. We have addresses of distant cousins and hope to find them and surprise them with an unexpected visit. It'll certainly be fun."

"Do you speak Italian?"

"My husband speaks a little. Michael, say a few words to the gentleman."

Michael obligingly complied with a short, prepared sentence but his accent was such that I could hardly understand a word he said.

"Mmmm.... Naples is not Cincinnati and you may have some trouble making yourself understood. Where are you staying?"

"In a little hotel we've been recommended."

She showed me a card with the hotel's name and address. The place was in one of Naples poorer areas and with their very obvious appearance and demeanour of American tourists, I gave the two sweet old people little chance of escaping the nasty tricks of young rascals after easy money.

"I hope you know that some parts of Naples can be rough, so try to avoid walking around with necklaces, watches, cameras, or a handbag. You might have problems."

"Oh! But we are Neapolitans," she said in earnest. "I am sure nobody would harm us."

"Apart from the fact that, much as you may feel like Neapolitans you certainly don't look local, your reasoning is akin to saying that in Downtown New York nobody would ever mug a New Yorker. Take it from me, be very careful!"

We landed in Naples, shook hands and went our separate ways.

The following day, I boarded the late afternoon flight back to Rome. The plane was nearly empty and I saw my American friends sitting forlornly in the middle of the aircraft.

"So, how did it go?"

I should never have asked. The old lady started to cry in her handkerchief and her husband, contrary to his amiable self, muttered ugly swear-words.

A taxi had taken them to the hotel and, as was to be expected, had shamelessly cheated them. The hotel was miserable and smelly and not at all what they had hoped for. They had left their suitcases there and gone in search of other accommodation but, not trusting the hotel personnel, had carried with them most of their money, their wallets and official papers in a small bag. A few minutes later, the passenger of a passing scooter had ripped the bag from Michael's hands and vanished into the traffic. Hoping to get some assistance from their local relatives, they had taken a taxi to their addresses. Alas, their fourth generation cousins had either moved or died and nobody could help them.

All this had been too much for them in such a short time. They had not even unpacked their bags and in the morning, after a night during which the sound of the romantic Neapolitan songs they had expected had been replaced by the din of racing motorcycles, they had returned to the airport and taken a flight to Rome on their way back to Cincinnati. They no longer felt like Neapolitans and reverted to what they had really been when they arrived, real Americans nurturing romantic dreams of a mythical primeval paradise. They will probably never return to Naples and, because of their own naivety, will have missed a wonderful experience.

This sad story offers a simple lesson to the naïve traveler. When in a foreign land, enthusiasm must leave some space for sober reflection and for facing up to the hard realities of the place. One must, above all, learn to be like a chameleon and completely blend in with the local crowd, rather than stand out like a sore thumb ready to be plucked like a sitting duck.

I will, for instance, never take my wife to some of the most fascinating areas in the Middle East, since the stubborn woman obstinately refuses to wear a black robe and cover her face with a veil!

The rewards of a few concessions may often be worth the effort....and Naples can be a delightful place.

WERNER'S DISCOVERY OF LIFE

Werner is an extremely successful businessman from Munich. In his early forties, he is enthusiastic, enterprising, and has the energy of a mad bull. He makes no bones about stating that during war time, his father had been a confirmed Nazi. Once in jest of doubtful taste, after a protracted negotiation, he declared that, had we met during the war, he would have taken great personal pleasure in baking me to a cinder! Despite these harsh assertions, we respect one another and our relations are very friendly.

Werner is an intensive workaholic. Up at six every morning, he starts with half an hour's exercise, followed by a shower and a hearty breakfast, before going to his office where he works without a break until eight at night.

He then returns to his charming wife, herself a reputed economist. During supper, they exchange political and financial information before going to bed for a well-deserved rest.

Werner travels extensively to supervise and control his offices worldwide and his factories in the Far East and South America. There is not a single minute wasted in his life and the notion of "holidays" and "hobbies" escape him completely. When faced with a problem, Werner shrugs it off with a simple statement:

"There is nothing money can't solve, and I make bucket loads of it every day."

The man has no children to hinder his life which is as straight as a rocket's path.

I deal with him both as a supplier and as a customer and the more he's got to know me, the more he is mesmerized by my character and lifestyle. My relaxed approach to business and the occasional joke I throw in to loosen the atmosphere during tense meetings always takes him by surprise and upsets his train of thought. I manage to spend time with my family, take holidays, play tennis, go skiing and even day-dream! My obvious enjoyment of these useless activities and the total waste of time they imply is a mystery to Werner who cannot understand how a man he rates as intelligent could so completely squander his life.

One evening, while having dinner with him in Germany, I grew exasperated by his conversation exclusively dedicated to business and made a bet with him:

"I will make you completely waste at least five hours of your precious time, and you will enjoy every minute of it. You will also thank me for it."

"Bob, you're out of your mind. You are taking an impossible gamble, but I'll give you three months to carry it out and prove your point."

Very demanding of himself and his people, Werner could be generous with those who performed well for his company. Sometime after this conversation, he unexpectedly asked me for some suggestions:

"Some of my managers have done a great job this year and I'd like to reward them with something else than just money. Any ideas?"

"Sure, bring them down to Naples. We'll take them for a visit to Pompeii and for a weekend in Capri."

He welcomed the idea but since, with Werner, generosity had its limits and nothing was ever wasted, he imposed a tight schedule with one day's business discussions and one day devoted to an efficiently organized and minutely timed guided tour.

The group arrived in Naples on a warm morning in June and after a harassing working day, we checked in at the hotel.

The ancient historical quarters of Naples probably offer the largest and certainly the most fascinating real-life museum in Europe. The busy medieval alleyways bustle with people who live and work in surroundings which date back many centuries. This is the realm of true Neapolitans with all their hospitality, exuberance and lust for life, chaos and mischief. I had often been warned by my local friends to keep well away from these dark alleys but found their charm so irresistible that nothing could stop me from strolling around.

The largest of these antique areas is the Spanish Quarter built by the Aragon kings for the sailors of their fleet during their domination of Naples. It was then notorious for its brothels, bandits, infamous bars, fights and murders. It is today the kingdom of artisans, old crafts and delightful traditions long forgotten in industrial countries.

Colorful garments and bed linen hang high across the streets to dry on ropes stretched between balconies, craftsmen toil on their open stalls and excitedly comment on their work with bystanders. Women cook in their kitchens for all to see while they watch the latest sitcoms on their TV's. Traditional Neapolitan songs escape from many windows and strollers cross themselves as they pass saintly statues along the streets. Small gatherings hotly argue over prices of contraband cigarettes and watches peddled by local smugglers while children look out for the police and pilfer anything they can from the unsuspecting bystanders. Riding three at a time, youngsters deafeningly race their supercharged scooters between the well accustomed pedestrians.

Traders loudly announce their arrival with sing-song calls while they slowly push their carts loaded with fruit, vegetables, household wares and other assorted goods along the narrow streets. Hanging at the end of ropes, empty baskets containing shopping lists scribbled on a piece of paper are lowered by women living on upper floors. Loud exchanges take place between the merchant filling the basket and the client while neighbors watch from their windows and comment on the proceedings. The quality of the fruit and vegetables is debated at length, highly praised by one side and disparaged by the other. Once the basket is full, it is hoisted back by the customer who carefully inspects every item. The money due is lowered to the merchant, only if the purchaser is fully satisfied otherwise the whole street echoes with loud protests and imprecations, each side heatedly defending its own interests.

The whole quarter is invaded by a rich perfume, an intimate blend of cooking, washing, olive and fish preserves, gasoline, sweat and, depending on the season, an infinite variety of stenches produced by the heaps of refuse bins awaiting collection.

I thought that the Spanish Quarter in Naples, so different from Werner's modern German town, would throw the man off guard and give me a good chance to win my bet.

As we walked from the hotel through the streets of present-day Naples, I told Werner the fascinating story of the ancient quarter we were about to visit.

"Akh!" he commented, "As usual your imagination runs wild!"

As we left via Toledo, the border between modern and old city, our surroundings changed abruptly. Werner watched, speechless and fascinated by the gigantic open theater around us which, until this moment, had only existed for him in the fantasy world of historical films.

We stopped at a small wine-tasting bar. Its walls were lined from floor to ceiling with ancient barrels which left no space for tables or chairs. Customers stood around the tiny bar where the owner served. As we entered, he handed us glasses from the first barrel. We toasted and drank. The wine was rich, fruity and full of the Mediterranean sunshine and perfumes which had fostered its growth. While I tasted the nectar in small sips, inhaling its rich aroma, Werner gulped it down and asked for a glass from another barrel. The shopkeeper gladly obliged but tried to explain to my friend that wine was not vodka and that one had to take time to enjoy it rather than swallow it in one swig. He amicably put his hand on Werner's forearm and, mimicking what he could not explain in words understandable to his host, gave a complete lesson in wine tasting. Walking to the door, he held up the glass against the light of the street lamp, admiring the color of the wine. Then, as if talking to a beautiful woman, he said with an inspired sigh:

"Bello… bello…bello!"

He let an angel pass, looked at Werner, handed him the glass and pointing his finger at him, said

"Now you!"

Werner held up the glass, gave it a quick glance and said, in quick succession:

"Bello, bello, bello!"

He then quizzically looked at his host, ready to drink, but the Italian shook his head in distress:

"No good, no good!"

He took the glass, held it up again and, with an inspired sigh, eyes half-closed as if getting ready for a declaration of love, he repeated with a voice vibrant with feeling and sentiment:

"Bello!"

Then shaking his head as if amazed by the unbelievable beauty of a work of art, he sighed deeply, looked sideways at Werner as if taking him in testimony, then slowly repeated:

"Bello! Bello!"

He returned the glass to Werner and upped his head to say:

"Now you!"

Conscious that every customer in the bar was following his movements, Werner had no choice but comply. As he concluded his inspired act, everybody clapped and cheered. Ready to gulp the reward of his effort, Werner brought the glass to his lips… but no! The shop owner stopped his arm and once again, took the glass, slowly rotated the wine it contained then brought it to his nostrils. He delicately inhaled as he would have done when smelling the perfume of a flower. After a pause, hands clasped around the glass as if in prayer, he lifted his face and looked around him in blissful daze. His rough, burrowed face looked like that of a saint in a primitive painting.

Werner's expression had slowly evolved from impatience to mesmerized amazement at the changes occurring on the older man's traits as if induced by some magic potion from a secret fountain of youth. A respectful silence reigned in the small wine shop as if a sacred ritual was being performed by a venerated high priest. The man handed the glass to Werner, inviting him to follow his example and learn the slow, patient and sacred art of wine tasting.

Now serious and concentrated, Werner looked like a humble student following his master's teachings. People held their breath while the foreign visitor inhaled the wine's perfume in light, fast whiffs. He opened his eyes and looked at the master with anxiety. A wave of relief passed through the bar as the older man smiled approvingly. As if moved by a common impulse, people in the shop formed a ring around the two men, held up their glass, gave a toast and drank in unison with much clicking of tongue and appreciative hums.

The old furrow-faced, beard-stubbed Neapolitan took his clean shaven and elegant foreign customer in his arms and hugged him affectionately. Werner returned the hug, unexpected emotional tears swelling in his eyes. A thunder of applause exploded and people came from neighboring shops to see what was causing the commotion. Werner would not leave until he had tasted and commented upon the wine from each barrel. I had never seen him in this mood and his managers watched him in wonder, amazed at the new man who had unexpectedly sprung to life.

Time had gone by and we were hungry.

I asked for the bill and prepared to pay but the owner looked at me with a hurt expression.

"No Signore, you won't affront me by paying. This evening is on the house. You will pay next time you come."

When I translated this for Werner, he was dumbfounded. The situation was beyond his experience and understanding. Why would the man give away his precious products and his time to strangers he did not know and would probably ever see again? But discussion was to no avail, the wine merchant would not accept our money.

I asked him to direct us to a good pizzeria. He took Werner's arm and led him down the road. With a wink of complicity to all in the shop, I put money on the counter and left. The ancient art of traditional hospitality and that of discreet reward for services rendered had both been carried out with grace.

The wine merchant took us to a tiny pizzeria and greeted his friend with a resounding "*Ciao Antò!*"

Antonio, the pizza cook, working with his long handled spatula retrieved, from the hearth, a beautifully brown pizza, its centre simmering with yellow mozzarella cheese, decorated with red tomatoes, pink cubes of bacon and green sage leaves. He placed his artwork on a plate, then exchanged a few words with the wine merchant who bade us good night and left us in the care of his friend.

Antonio announced the long list of different pizzas he could serve, but we ordered the ancestor of them all, pizza Margherita.

He started making his dough. Alive and compliant in his nimble hands, the lump quickly changed shape from a round globe to a long roll then back again to a ball before it became a perfectly round thin disc, ready to hold the cheese and tomatoes which would cover its surface.

Werner watched him intently. Aware of his customer's gaze, Antonio invited him to stand by the counter then, as if inspired by a sudden thought, he presented him with a round ball of dough:

"*Tua pizza*," he said.

Werner smiled.

"*Bello, bello*," he answered as the wine merchant had taught him.

Encouraged, Antonio put the dough in Werner's hands and helped him to knead it. At first taken aback, Werner warmed to the game, worked hard and produced a perfect pizza base. Antonio covered it with cheese and tomatoes, and placed it in the oven while Werner watched the baking of his pizza intently. We ate, intoxicated by the wine and the warmth of the hearth. A mellow numbness invaded us all and, after finishing our supper, we slowly ambled towards our hotel through the narrow streets of the Spanish Quarter.

The lightness of the early summer air gave the impression of floating rather than walking to the Town Hall square. We stopped to admire the view. The massive towers of the Angiovine castle dominated the area, the sea scintillated in the distance under the silvery light of a full moon and Mount Vesuvius imposingly stood guard on the bay.

Werner stopped, inhaled deeply and sat on one of the benches facing the castle and the sea. He leaned back and stretching like a contented cat, folded his arms behind his head. Unlike the fast talking and ever-twitching man I knew, he sat quietly, absorbing the midnight scene of Naples around him. Oblivious to their surroundings, two lovers were kissing languorously on one of the benches, hands unashamedly exploring their hungry bodies, a lonely man sat on another bench, daydreaming while a pack of stray dogs playing hide and seek were amicably sniffing each other's' backsides. Time went by slowly in the magic of a dreamy and still moment of midnight in Naples.

Werner came close to me, making sure his managers could not hear him:

"Akh Napoli...," he said in confidence then fell silent again.

"Well, Werner, how does it feel to have been doing nothing for the past few hours?"

He took some time to answer:

"I think I have learned a great deal tonight and I am very sorry to admit that I am ready to have more evenings like this. You and your Neapolitan poison! I should have known better than to come! Now I start to understand why, though always full of brilliant ideas, Italians are often late in delivery, poor in service and forgetful of details. Who cares if people wait! Why worry! Things will always be all right in the end."

His tone suddenly changed:

"Nah! That's enough! I'm getting stupid. Let's go back to the hotel."

Werner was never the same again. A few days later, his wife phoned in alarm:

"What have you done to him? I don't know my husband anymore."

Shortly after his visit, Werner bought a little retreat in the Black Forest where, for the first time in his life, he took a two week vacation without telephones, computers or business meetings.

The busy man had finally discovered in nonchalant Naples the taste of *"dolce farniente"*, generous human warmth and earthly paradise.

RAINDROPS FROM CLEAR SKIES

The day at the office had been long and difficult. Disagreements among the three company owners had resulted in heated, emotional and inconclusive discussions. I was glad to be back at the hotel and relax on the balcony, admiring the bay of Naples and Mount Vesuvius.

A trip to the volcano's crater would quickly reveal the hard and cruel reality of its nature and give a good idea of Dante's Inferno. Chaotic rivers of frozen black lava cover the mountain's flanks in a vision of destruction and desolation. The bottom of the deep and awesome crater is blocked by huge boulders of basalt and a thick crust of black dust. The entrails of the earth are not far and the mountain appears as if crouched in wait, preparing for the next gigantic explosion to clean the surrounding area of its mocking and carefree people who defiantly invade its slopes.

On that pleasant evening, the golden rays of sunset caressed the top of the mountain and light clouds embraced it within woolly pink and mauve shawl.

Joyous street noises beckoned, and I left my room for a stroll in the city.

At one point, the seaside avenue divides in two: one half follows the shore while the other gently slopes up towards Piazza Plebiscito, a vast piazza in front of the royal palace, surrounded by a beautiful colonnade. The edge of the sloping avenue is lined with a marble parapet

Business Travel Can Be Fun

supported by small columns. The harmony of shapes and the beauty of the scenery invite the stroller to stop and daydream.

I sat on a bench, admiring the scenery. A cheerful group of children were running up and down the edge of the road along the parapet. From time to time, they would all crouch behind the small columns and giggle uncontrollably. One of them was holding what appeared to be a long cylindrical stick. They would stop every so often, place the stick between two of the columns and, while one of them stood up holding it against his belly, the others would look down on the other side of the parapet. They then would all crouch again and laugh hysterically. A few minutes later, they would all get up, run to another point and start the whole game again.

I tried to see what was making them laugh but, from my bench, try as I might, I couldn't understand. I got up, walked to the edge of the parapet and looked down. On the pavement, some ten meters below, people were sitting in an open-air café, chatting in front of their drinks. I still couldn't see the reason for the children's mirth. They were now getting up from one of their periodic crouching and hiding sessions and I watched them, pretending not to look at their obviously mischievous game.

What, from afar, appeared to be a stick was a long hollow cardboard tube. The child who was holding it would unzip his trousers and with great concentration put his little penis into the tube, deftly positioning it between two columns then, with obvious enjoyment, he would pee into the tube while his young friends over the parapet observed the reactions of the coffee drinkers below. The drops took a few moments to reach their sitting targets and during that time, the young pisser would end his session and quickly pull the tube out of view.

The idea was certainly astute and full of fun. I also watched the reactions below. As the few drops fell from the cloudless skies, the surprised coffee drinkers would look up, wondering where the water had come from. Seeing nothing, they would just wipe their bald heads and their table with their hands and, unconcerned, go back to their conversations and their drinks.

This, of course, sent the kids into hysterics; the idea of pissing, without being caught on fat, carefree bourgeois craniums, was for them the best joke of the century! There were only six children, so the game soon had to stop for lack of ammunition.

Good people, when you intend to sit peacefully on the sunny veranda of an open café, check first that there aren't any uncontrolled children running around somewhere above your head!

HIS LORDSHIP'S BUS TRIP BACK TO TOWN

Some years ago, the Neapolitan government decided to liven up the area with a summer festival. Its various events would certainly attract tourists from all over the world if they took place in some of the region's many wonderful historical monuments. Which of these would be best suited for plays and concerts? The beautiful ruins of Pompeii? Too dangerous! People could get lost in the town's ancient back streets or worse, try to rekindle the Roman orgies in the miraculously preserved town brothel, beautifully adorned with its original paintings of most inventive Bacchanalian debauchery. The courtyards of Naples's medieval and Renaissance castles? These were already well known and had often hosted earlier festivals. Something new had to be found.

The province of Naples has a vast collection of patrician mansions, built through the centuries by noblemen, rich merchants and early industrialists. Many of these beautiful estates had been donated to the State by the descendants of rich families who could no longer afford their upkeep, repair or high taxes. Abandoned to their fate and ruined by abusive dwellers, these decayed villas, once restored, offered ideal settings for art festivals. The extraordinary but sadly short-lived "Festival of Pompeian Villas" was thus born in 1990.

That July evening when I left the office, the air was warm and the sun was still high in the sky. I looked at the evening's entertainment program and fell upon this festival which I had never heard of. I asked the hotel porter for directions but he scoffed at the idea. The festival, he said, was miles away out of town and he was outraged by the large sums of good taxpayers' money which had been spent to restore the tumbled down old houses for the enjoyment of the rich and privileged. Having abundantly vented his displeasure, he finally informed me that the closest mansion which featured a play was half an hour's train ride away, followed by another half hour's walk. No taxi, he said, would take me to this godforsaken place.

It took me a long time to reach Campolieto, a beautiful eighteenth-century estate. Waiting for the play to start, the public sat facing the sea, respectfully admiring the sunset.

Darkness slowly fell and the play started under the moon's silvery glow. At the end of the performance, well past midnight, people got into their cars and left. I walked back to the train station but found it closed with no trains scheduled at this late hour. I waited for a taxi but none came so, at one o'clock in the morning, I walked back to the villa and asked the night porter to please call a cab.

"A cab, Sir? But there are no cabs at this time. You may be able to catch a night bus at the station just outside our gates."

"How frequently does it pass?"

"I don't know, maybe once every two hours!"

By that time, all spectators who could have taken me back to town had irretrievably left so I had no choice but to wait. I tried to hitchhike, but this proved a total waste of a good thumb's time since very few cars were passing and none was foolish enough to stop for an unknown stranger. At last the bus came.

It was an old double-coach vehicle driven by an old man. As aged as his driving mate, the ticket collector limped on one leg. They were probably two retired pensioners and the only team to accept night work on that route. I was the only passenger in the large vehicle and sat right behind the driver. I paid my thirty cents fare to Naples and listened distractedly to the two men complaining of the hardness of times, the incompetence of government, the uselessness of the workers' unions and the laziness and ignorance of the young... nothing different from an ordinary conversation between honest, hard working old-timers the world over.

Three stations further on, the bus was waived to a stop by the imperative arm of a young man. The driver opened the door to the youngster who got in and walked hurriedly past the conductor all the way to the far end of the second coach.

"Hey you!" called the ticket collector, "Come back here and pay your fare. Can't you see where I'm standing? Why didn't you stop instead of running to the back? Do we stink or something? Are you too good for us or are we slaves to you? Have you no respect for your elders, young man?"

Business Travel Can Be Fun

Hearing no answer, I turned round. The youngster was unconcernedly looking out of the window and had obviously no intention of moving. Muttering and swearing under his breath, the conductor hopped on his valid leg to the back of the bus. The machine clanged along on the uneven road while the driver hummed a Neapolitan tune.

All of a sudden, we heard raised voices and angry words. The young man shouted at the conductor:

"No, I won't pay. Not for feeding old farts like you and your driving mate or for the upkeep of this old, tumbledown heap of rubbish. You have the nerve to call this a bus? It's a scrap-heap just good enough for old goats, for donkeys and for decrepit slaves of the thieving government! I will not pay."

"Stop Angelo!" called the conductor to the driver, "let's get this bastard off the bus."

"I will not leave," yelled back the young man. "Get me out of here if you can, you old maggot!"

I looked at my watch: three fifteen in the morning! If this went on much longer, apart from a hysterically funny dialogue in Neapolitan slang, I would get nothing for my night, no sleep, no rest, nothing! We were stopped in a no-win situation. I walked to the back of the bus and addressed the conductor:

"Look Sir, perhaps this young man has had a difficult evening. I will pay for his fare so that we can resume our journey and keep to your schedule."

I handed him the money. He looked at me, then at the young man:

"It's because of this gentleman's kindness that I will let you stay on the bus. I don't know why he does this because you certainly don't deserve it! Come on Angelo, let's get moving. The gentleman paid for this rascal's fare."

The bus slowly started to move, the conductor hopped back to the front, I briefly winked and smiled at the sulky young man, glad to have solved the problem, and went back to my seat.

Moments later, I was startled by the youngster who tapped on my shoulder. As I looked up, he loudly cleared his throat, dramatically knelt next to me in the aisle of the bus and spoke as if to a large audience with tremolos in his voice and theatrical waving of arms:

"Thank you sir for your kindness and for your generosity. I gather from your accent that you are not from this land of heathens. I can however sense in you a great mind and a generous heart which recognise a man's nobility of soul and understand and value the virtues of poets and artists. Not like these two cretins who, because they drive a bus and collect fares think that they are the masters of the world instead of seeing themselves for what they really are, confounded imbeciles and lackeys of the rotten government of this country!"

A loud screeching of brakes sent the young man rolling on the floor and projected me against the glass window which separated me from the driver. The bus doors flew open with a clang:

"Get off the bus at once you son of the mother of whores!" screamed the driver as he tried to kick the man.

Fast as a monkey, the youngster sprung to his feet, ran to the back of the bus while pulling faces and mimicking the horns of the devil with two forefingers on top of his head.

"Come and get me you old farts, come and get me if you can!"

This was too much for the driver. As fast as his old legs could carry him, he hobbled to the back closely followed by the limping conductor. As soon as they got close to him, the youngster jumped off the back door, ran along the pavement to the front and jumped back in the bus pulling out his tongue, making faces, and rolling his eyes in simulated terror.

"Silly old farts, silly old farts, he chanted as he sat in the driver's seat and continuously hooted the horn."

He then sprang out of the bus and vanished in the dark.

The driver and the conductor screamed obscene insults at him. Lights came on in the surrounding houses, people opened their windows:

"Shut up, you idiots!"

"We'll call the police if you don't stop this row!"

"Drunken drivers again! This is what our government does with our money, waste it on old degenerates which they call Civil Servants."

The driver and his colleague tried to justify themselves but soon beaten and dejected, the two old men painfully heaved themselves back on the bus and we slowly pulled away, clanging and bumping our way on the chaotic road back to Naples.

The conductor sat next to me, tears welling up in his eyes;

"This is what you get for your efforts! There is no more respect for honest people!" he sighed. "The only way to survive today in this country is through abuse, theft, drug dealing and pimping. Ah! Poor Italy! Where are you going to Sir?"

It was close to four in the morning and the question took a moment to register.

"To the Hotel Jolly in Naples but this is way off your route so I'll get off as soon as we see a taxi rank."

"Nah! Close or far makes no difference. After what we've suffered together, we cannot abandon you in the middle of nowhere at this time of night! We'll take you to your hotel."

And so I was dropped in lordly fashion in front of my hotel door, the only passenger of a regional night bus driven by two kind elderly gentlemen who felt they owed a friendly foreigner a personal apology for the misbehaviour and abuse of a youngster unworthy of Naples' ancient tradition of hospitality and graciousness!

The bus ride had beaten by far the entertainment offered by the Festival of Pompeian Villas.

CHAPTER 6

TWO LADIES

Someone could possess everything and have nothing. Others can find everything in nothing.

A ROUGH LIFE!

I boarded the flight on a sunny morning and quickly sat down to resume my reading, oblivious to the shuffling of the other passengers. Somebody sat next to me and a rich scent of perfume soon invaded the area. Too absorbed by the hilarious story I was reading, I finished my paragraph and laughed loud as I looked up.

"Your book appears great fun!"

My very pretty neighbour was in her thirties, expensively dressed and magnificently made up. On her lap were a little white bag and a white toy poodle, whose startled eyes were darting anxiously around.

"Yes indeed, it is extremely funny. I highly recommend it."

"Oh thanks! I need a laugh after the two weeks I've just had!"

Sensing that the lady needed to unburden her woes, I encouraged her:

Business Travel Can Be Fun

"Rough time?"

"Terrible! I'm glad it's over but dread what's coming! Life is so difficult for me at the moment!"

"Lots of work?"

"Don't ask! A living hell! It's my ex-husband. We're still good friends, but I really had to divorce. I couldn't stand our life anymore! You see, he owns a famous wine Château in France. Because of the heavy taxes and high salaries in the country, he bought a huge plot of land in Argentina where he also grows grapes and makes wine. Up to our separation, we lived six months in France and the other six in Argentina, and in both places I worked like a slave to entertain his friends. I spent my days receiving noblemen, ministers, and millionaires of all kinds with exacting demands, impossible whims and kinky fantasies. I had an army of servants to manage, five houses to upkeep, and did not have a day's rest. When I wasn't entertaining, I was being entertained in New-York, Paris or elsewhere and always had to smile and be in a good mood. I'd had enough of this life, so last year I asked for a divorce and got it. My husband is very understanding about these things."

I looked at her, trying to find an intelligent comment to make about her ghastly life, but she went on without a pause.

"I admit he was generous and left me an apartment on the Avenue Foch in Paris, another on the Via Veneto in Rome, a house in Geneva and a house in Nice. My present problem is that I have to return all his family's ancestral furniture and replace it with something more to my taste. This is the reason why I am really exhausted. Two weeks ago I was at an auction sale in Sotheby's in New York; last week I spent two days at Christies' in London, then went to Paris. I came yesterday to Geneva and am now going to

Rome to discuss the decoration of the apartment with my architect. To top it all, I found that out that last week, my poor Linda, my dog, had a disagreement with the Paris apartment housekeeper whom she hates, and bit her hand! I had to dismiss the housekeeper and take Linda with me. I am now left with no housekeeper in Paris and when I return next week, the apartment will no doubt be so dusty that I'll have to go to a hotel until I find somebody to clean it! Oh! I really can't take it anymore; it's just too much for me!"

Sobs welled up in her throat forcing her to stop speaking. She looked at me, her eyes filling up with tears of utter misery.

"This is why it's so good for me to hear you laugh when you read your book. I need to laugh and to feel carefree and happy again!"

Had we been standing, my first reaction would have been to take her in my arms and comfort her as one would do with a little girl who had just broken her doll. Under the circumstances, I was relieved to see the air hostess bringing the breakfast trays.

Life, I thought, was indeed difficult for this poor young woman. No doubt the beautiful but melancholic lady and her sweet poodle had an impossibly hard time in Rome's Oh- so-miserable Via Veneto apartment.

It was, thank Heavens, easier for me with just one little house and a wife who moaned because she felt that we needed to change our twenty year old sofa on which the children, in their earlier years, had dropped their coffee and cream and on which India, our shaggy mongrel, had left the marks of its dirty paws after a happy run in the garden mud!

———

A HAPPY DAY TO YOU!

A few days later, the sun was already shining above Cairo when I drew back the curtains of my room at the Hilton Hotel. It was six thirty in the morning and the noble river Nile glimmered under Egypt's clear sky. The huge town was still free from its cloud of pollution and one could perceive in the distance the imposing outline of the pyramids.

I dressed, had breakfast, and instead of taking a taxi to my Agent's office, decided to walk across Ramses Square to the city's business district.

In my grey suit, white shirt and blue tie with my attaché case in hand, I stopped for a moment to look at sparrows fighting in the dust over crumbs of bread thrown to them by an elderly woman sitting on the ground. Of fair complexion, she wore an ample robe which covered her completely except for her face and feet. Her dyed red hair cascading over her shoulders gave her the air of an ancient gipsy foreign to the surroundings.

A newspaper used as a napkin was spread in front of her with a piece of flat unleavened Egyptian bread on it, a heap of sliced onions, an aluminium plate full of black beans and a tin can of water. She obviously relished her breakfast and ostentatiously, with slow movements, picked up a piece of bread between her not very clean thumb, index and middle finger, dipped it in the rich black beans and stuffed the lot deep in her wide open mouth with the contented expression of somebody eating a rare delicacy.

She looked up at me, her green eyes twinkling with delight. I could not help but smile back and, in Arabic, wished her "Bon appétit and God bless your day." She stopped munching in surprise while I resumed my walk across the square.

"Hey Mister!" she called after me, "come and share my breakfast."

Having opened the exchange, I could not be so rude as not to answer so I turned round and said without stopping:

"I'm sorry kind Mother but I must rush."

A few seconds later, naked feet pattered behind me and my hand was gripped by oily fingers. She looked at me her green eyes shining in earnest.

"You can't insult me by not eating with me," she said out of breath. "You must share my breakfast, I insist you must!"

There was no escape. The woman was old, small, shrivelled and obviously very poor but she had an air of dignity and immense kindness in her manners.

I returned with her to her spread newspaper and, in my grey suit, white shirt and blue tie, sat in the dust next to her.

She gave me half her bread and ordered:

"Eat! You're too thin! You are not being properly looked after!"

Although imperfect, my Arabic was sufficient to allow a simple conversation.

Of Greek origin, Elena's family had settled in Egypt a long time ago. They had suffered a reversal of fortune and late in life, she found herself alone and penniless which did not seem to unduly worry her as she lived happily, day by day.

God had given, God had taken back. Blessed be Him who gave her bread, water and a day of sunshine!

After eating my bread and beans, I waited for her to finish her breakfast, thanked her and handed her some money. She haughtily refused. I helped her gather her paper, aluminium bowl and tin can which she carefully placed in an old bag. She thanked me for my company, wished me a happy day and walked off with an air of tired dignity.

I had received a great lesson in the art of happiness, humility, and love of life.

What more could a traveller ever hope for?

CONCLUSION

Travel! An activity which has always drawn and fascinated mankind. Throughout history, it has been, and still is, a major source of our species' cultural wealth.

When abroad, we are often surprised by the many common values we share with foreigners whom, prior to meeting them, we thought to be totally alien to us.

Where differences are deep, travel invites us to understand, accept, and sometimes even integrate some of this "otherness" in our own behavior. When this happens, it can often be a great source of personal fulfillment.

Wherever one goes, one finds wonderful folks, each with their own qualities and defects. In faraway places, they may have a different sense of humor, eat differently or dance in other ways, but human beings, the world over, are endowed with the blessing of knowing how to smile, laugh, dance and be merry! Our personal challenge and opportunity is to understand how to elicit the best out of the individuals we meet and, in return, to share with them the better side of us. It can be an infinite source of mutual satisfaction.

Wonderful travel adventures never stop. One can deliberately set them up or happen upon them, but, taken with a sense of humor and humility, whether positive or adverse, they will always offer a wealth of education and adventure.

May all your travels, whether for business or pleasure, always be a source of personal enrichment, delight…and, above all, fun.

www.ingramcontent.com/pod-product-compliance
Lightning Source LLC
Chambersburg PA
CBHW022106040426
42451CB00007B/149